Meditations
FOR THE
SOUL

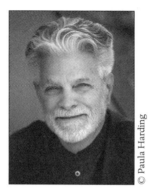
© Paula Harding

ABOUT THE AUTHOR

Neale Lundgren, PhD, is a therapist, former Benedictine monk, poet, and musician. He received his doctoral degree from Emory University in psychological, philosophical, and religious thought and has taught courses at St. John's University, Emory University, and Pacifica Graduate Institute. As a teacher, he uses the conversation of presence, reflective reading, meditation, and transformational energy work to help put students in touch with the sacred. Neale lives in Atlanta, Georgia. Visit him online at www.nealelundgren.com.

Meditations

FOR THE

SOUL

NEALE LUNDGREN PhD

Llewellyn Publications
Woodbury, Minnesota

First Edition
First Printing, 2020

Cover design by Shannon McKuhen
Editing by Laura Kurtz

Llewellyn Publications is a registered trademark of Llewellyn
Worldwide Ltd.

Library of Congress Cataloging-in-Publication Data
Names: Lundgren, Neale, author
Title: Meditations for the soul / Neale Lundgren.
Description: First edition. | Woodbury, Minnesota : Llewellyn
  Publications, [2020] | Includes bibliographical references. | Summary:
  "Meditations from Eastern and Western spiritual traditions for
  enlightenment"— Provided by publisher.
Identifiers: LCCN 2020031293 (print) | LCCN 2020031294 (ebook) |
  ISBN 9780738764306 (paperback) | ISBN 9780738766980 (ebook)
Subjects: LCSH: Meditation. | Yoga. | Soul. | Mind and body.
Classification: LCC BL627 .L85 2020 (print) | LCC BL627 (ebook) |
  DDC 204/.32—dc23
LC record available at https://lccn.loc.gov/2020031293
LC ebook record available at https://lccn.loc.gov/2020031294

Llewellyn Worldwide Ltd. does not participate in, endorse, or have any authority or responsibility concerning private business transactions between our authors and the public.

All mail addressed to the author is forwarded but the publisher cannot, unless specifically instructed by the author, give out an address or phone number.

Any internet references contained in this work are current at publication time, but the publisher cannot guarantee that a specific location will continue to be maintained. Please refer to the publisher's website for links to authors' websites and other sources.

Llewellyn Publications
A Division of Llewellyn Worldwide Ltd.
2143 Wooddale Drive
Woodbury, MN 55125-2989
www.llewellyn.com

Printed in the United States of America

FORTHCOMING BOOKS
BY NEALE LUNDGREN PHD

Meditations for the Soul, volume 2:
Guide Map for the Inner Traveler

The Ruby Cup, a novel based on
Dr. Lundgren's monastery journey.

The Teaching, a novella that illuminates the teachings
of universal wisdom.

Across the Threshold, an exploration into the mystical
states and stages of consciousness in the
esoteric traditions of the world religions.

DEDICATION

To the Awakener, Meher Baba,
and to all sincere seekers this book may one day find.

The deeper secrets of spiritual life
are unraveled to those who take risks
and who make bold experiments with it.
—*Meher Baba*

Contents

Part Three
BRINGING SOUL TO THE MATERIAL WORLD

Introduction

EVERYONE IS A SEEKER. Everyone longs for a soulful purpose that sets the heart ablaze. Even though we may be unaware of it, we are always seeking for what will bring joy and fulfillment to every fiber of our being. We are seeking to make sense of life. But we will find it difficult to make sense of life until we have made sense of the soul.

Making sense of the soul is awakening to the fact that the only real experience we ever have is of the immediate and irrefutable now. Our material mind pulls us to the regretful past and the worrisome future. Our soul mind gives us access to joyful presence. Learning ways to connect with the now, with presence, is essential for a fulfilled life.

In addition to the physical senses of sight, hearing, taste, smell, and touch are vibrant senses within the soul. When any of the soul's senses are activated, we become more present. It is presence that empowers us to navigate the inner and outer worlds of the spiritual and the everyday with confidence.

The purpose of this book is threefold: to provide you with ways to connect your body and mind to the senses of your soul; to give you strengthening practices and pathways for your soul's journey through the material world; and to impart to you teachings based on ancient wisdom that will help you bring more soulfulness to your relationships with others.

Your soul knows what you need to make you happy. Because of this, the direction of your soul may shift and change your life in ways you would have never expected. The soul does not move in straight lines. When the soul speaks, it often gives no clear answer, but says to us, "Seek and you will find."

My personal search to find and make sense of the soul began long ago. In my youth, I was a professional musician and singer, at the threshold of worldly success and fame. Overcome with the feeling that my life was empty and without meaning, I began to read every book of substance I could get my hands on. Although I didn't know it then, I'd lost a sense of soulful purpose. After abandoning my career in music, I decided to enroll as a student in philosophy at a nearby university.

Since the semester wouldn't begin for months, I felt compelled to go somewhere far away, anywhere that would take me from the soulless path I was on. Without hardly any money in our pockets, a friend and I set out on a hitch-hiking trek through Europe and North Africa.

One night, after reaching Orleans from Paris, the freezing temperatures of winter forced us to find a place where we might escape the cold. We came upon a monastery, located along the banks of the Loire River. We were immediately taken in, given room and board for two days and nights. Without speaking hardly a word the entire time we were there, we took meals with the monks and sat with them as they chanted ancient songs and meditated in silence.

On the morning of our departure, with a smile, along with bread and fruit for our journey, the guest master signaled to us a heartfelt goodbye. That brief but powerful experience would forever alter the course of my life.

Upon my return home, I decided that a monastery might be a school where I could find a spiritual teacher that would help me reconnect with my soul. This search led me to an abbey near the Great Lakes. Built in the early nineteenth century by German immigrants, seekers from all cultures were welcome as long as they were committed to follow the monastic path.

Life as a monk included a daily round of work and prayer. We were taught how to cultivate a meditative mind by immersing ourselves in studies on the soul. Stewardship

of the forest, farm fields, and spring-fed lakes that sur-
rounded the cloister kept a monk's soul close to the land
and its seasons.

Living closer to the soul of nature, I discovered a
rhythm where my own soul took the lead in the dance of
life. I established a regular practice of attentive breathing
into the heart and learned to listen from an inner place of
silence.

Meditation taught me about the nature of the self, the
nature of the soul, and how these were two distinct enti-
ties. Self-observation awakened me to the matrix of the
canned programs my lower mind had unwittingly absorbed.
Meditative breathing eventually gave me an experience of
my essential being. I sensed within me, within everyone
and all creation, a loving and aware presence. This breath
moving within me possessed its own intelligence. I've come
to call it warm consciousness, because it emits the distinct
qualities of pure love and resplendent light.

Although my monastery experiences took me ever more
inward to the depths of my being, after a number of years of
seeking within, it became clear to me that I must return to
the outside world. I wasn't sure what this would entail, since
I had gotten used to living in a cloistered setting.

It didn't take long before the busyness of life muted
the senses of my soul that I had become attuned to as a
monk. In effect, I had become a human doing rather than

a human being. It took me years to recover how to be fully human, to live from a soul-centered place in the midst of worldly activity.

I eventually became a psychotherapist and soon found that the spiritual tools I'd learned as a monk helped clients deal more effectively with life's problems. Now, thirty years later, I've come to understand the reason for my monastery experience: to assist others in the world seeking meaningful purpose for their lives by making sense of their souls.

To begin this journey with me, you do not need to pack a suitcase, purchase airfare, or reserve lodging. Although finding a place of minimal noise is certainly preferable, it is not essential. Just bring a spirit of openness to your inner search. If you want, you can call this your breathing room strategy. A breathing room is essentially an attitude of inner spaciousness. Your breathing room is your home base, the starting point for your journey inward.

This inner room can be as simple or as elaborate as you wish to make it. Visible only to you, it can be an open space with windows or a cozy chamber hidden away from the world. Make your breathing room comfortable, safe, and color it with your own sense of beauty, perhaps with an object or two that holds meaning for you.

Each chapter is designed to prepare you for a soul journey that includes a meditation practice as well as an awakening exercise. My particular approach to these soul journeys is interactive. They incorporate breath techniques, visualizations, and affirmations. I encourage you to bring your imagination and intuition to the process.

The soul remains intangible when viewed intellectually, from a distance. My intent is to provide you with helpful directives for tangible experiences of soul. Your soul was meant to breathe through your body, heart, and mind. You are the instrument through which the breath of your soul can play its beautiful music.

PART ONE
Awakening to Soul in the Material World

WHEN YOU WERE FIRST a child, your soul had already imprinted its identity upon you. You were awake. There was no division between your body, mind, heart, and soul. You were whole, one being. Your being was earthly and heavenly, full of bliss from the hair on your head to your toes. All of life was a sacred journey.

You may not recall the memory of it, but at some point you lost the natural delight of your being. As you grew up, the split between your soul's essence and your physical body widened. The gap between earth and heaven also grew larger.

Know that this phenomenon occurred only in your mind; falling from paradise is all part of the soul's journey. And you must make your way not back, but within.

It matters little when, where, or how the distortion of who you are came to be. At some point in your life, a faulty self-perception disconnected your physical senses of sight, hearing, taste, touch, and smell from the higher senses of your soul.

Your inner capacities of knowing have only receded and need to be coaxed out into the open air once again. You will find that once you have reawakened to your soul, your inner senses will be invigorated and you will become more present to your life.

The path to joy is living in this world from the vantage point of the soul. Your soul will give you belief in yourself and knowledge of yourself, knowledge of the fact that you are a creative force in and for the world.

Once you begin to identify more with your soul, life becomes imbued also with more meaning and purpose. The material world becomes a gold mine as opposed to a minefield. Only the soul knows that to be human is less a given than it is an achievement, an opportunity.

What awaits you is a story you are meant to write, a song you are meant to sing. Your inherited self is not the composer of your life. The true composer of your life is your individual soul. But first, you have to make sense of it. Once you do, your soul will breathe new life into you, a song waiting to begin again.

CHAPTER 1
Soul Therapy

YOU ARE OPENING THESE pages to get on course again with the direction of your soul. All you need is the desire to establish a lasting and positive connection with your essence and your soul therapy has already begun.

A number of pages of joy and sorrow have already been written upon your heart. Perhaps you sometimes suffer with worry, anxiety, or depression. A job you loved or an intimate relationship may have ended, and you don't know how to move on with a positive spirit. Someone near and dear to you might be dying or has already left this world of shadow and light and you wonder how you will go on without them or how to understand the riddle of death and its important role in life.

Your soul is that dimension of you that welcomes every human experience, all life's ups and downs, as the roller coaster ride it signed up for. Only your soul can take everything in stride because only your soul is large enough and present enough to make intelligent sense of the absurd world without giving up in despair.

When you expand your inner being you increase the potentials of human experience. Your soul possesses this innate ability, because your soul by its nature is a grand becoming that is meant to learn and unfold within the material world.

The lower mind experiences the material world of objects, nature, things, and people as something to be possessed, controlled, used, and discarded. This mind also filters the material world it partially perceives through feelings, thoughts, prejudices, and beliefs.

The soul, however, is your higher mind. This mind makes possible the inward journey in the midst of the material world. The soul is an expansive intelligence that can make sense of everything within and around you.

When every sense of your soul is finally activated, you will be better able to take in every experience as a means to enlarge and enliven your higher being. You will perceive every event of your life more exuberantly and loaded with meaning and purpose.

Your soul is the inner physician, the great healer who makes what has been divided in you whole again. You will awaken to the healing work your soul can accomplish once your soul's senses have been opened. Doing so will enable you to experience life far beyond the capacity of your material mind and its limited senses of sight, taste, smell, hearing, and touch.

A good place to start is with the soul's sense of touch. Your soul is actually closer to you than your physical body. This is not a concept but a felt reality. True knowing is in the experience.

In soul journey 1, you are invited to activate your soul's sense of touch through an experience of warm consciousness. See what happens when you enliven your ordinary breath with the intentional power of intelligent kindness. Warm consciousness provides you with soulful touch. When used often, this exercise will cleanse your mind of negativity.

After activating warm consciousness, you may begin to feel a pull from within. This key opens the portal to the vast being of your soul.

An important note about the soul journeys: After you read each sentence, feel free to close your eyes to enhance the experience, then open them again, and then proceed to the next instruction. Do this with every soul journey provided at the end of each chapter.

SOUL JOURNEY 1
Activating Warm Consciousness

MEDITATION

Find a quiet place. Sit comfortably. Close your eyes, and visualize your breathing room, that safe haven, with you inside it.

Relax the tension in your eyes, mouth, jaw, shoulders, chest, and stomach. Place your tongue gently on the roof of your mouth. This enables you to inhale and exhale through your nose easily. Follow the natural rhythm of your breath. Bring your awareness to the rise and fall of your breath as your stomach expands when you inhale and contracts when you exhale.

Open yourself to all sounds, sights, and smells that might come into your physical orbit. Without judgment, accept all thoughts that come into your mind and all feelings that may register in your body. Do this for as short or long a time as you wish.

AWAKENING EXERCISE

Bring your attention to the in and out flow of your breath throughout your body. Recall a time when you were inwardly touched by someone who gave you kindness when you were in need of it or when you gave to another the touch of your soul through the warmth of understanding.

Contribute this powerful ingredient of kindness to your awareness as you follow your breath. Do this consciously for a few rounds of breaths.

Now, imagine a small golden light in the center of your chest. Do not worry if you don't happen to feel anything yet. Just know that you have now permanently activated your soul's sense of touch: warm consciousness.

Return to this exercise often. Consider this your ignition key.

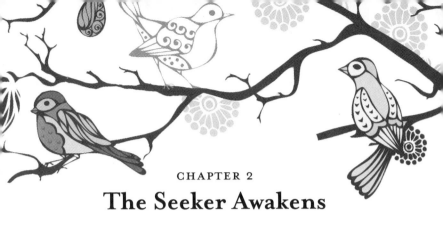

CHAPTER 2
The Seeker Awakens

THE SEEKER'S JOURNEY PROCEEDS in gradual awakenings, along with many stages and trials. There are questions you can ask yourself to help you figure out where you might be. There are, of course, no right or wrong answers. Let these serve as useful indicators of the adventure of soul that lies ahead.

SEEKER STAGE QUESTIONNAIRE

1. Do you feel like you are caught up in the whirlwind of the material world?

   Yes, more than No ____ No, more than Yes____

2. Do you tend to put your focus on worldly status and sometimes worried that you will not succeed?

   Yes, more than No ____ No, more than Yes____

3. Do you feel pressure from authority figures to think in a certain way?

Yes, more than No _____ No, more than Yes_____

4. Do you mostly rely on the approval of others?

Yes, more than No_____ No, more than Yes _____

5. Do you sometimes feel that you are living someone else's life and not your own?

Yes, more than No _____ No, more than Yes_____

6. Have you ever questioned your thoughts, beliefs and culturally based attitudes?

Yes, more than No _____ No, more than Yes _____

7. Do you tend to rebel against being told what to think or what to believe in?

Yes, more than No _____ No, more than Yes_____

8. Do you often argue with what others claim to be real or unreal, true or false?

Yes, more than No _____ No, more than Yes _____

9. Does it seem easier to see what is not true for you than what is true?

Yes, more than No _____ No, more than Yes _____

10. Do you tend to be pessimistic or dwell on the negative?

Yes, more than No _____ No, more than Yes _____

11. Do you have a desire to learn from different cultures and are likely to be influenced by some of their preferences, tastes, and customs?

Yes, more than No _____ No, more than Yes _____

12. Do you embrace cultural diversity?

    Yes, more than No _____ No, more than Yes _____

13. Are you more open to thinking differently about things than not?

    Yes, more than No _____ No, more than Yes _____

14. Do you have a desire to broaden your ideas about religion and spirituality?

    Yes, more than No _____ No, more than Yes _____

15. Are you welcoming toward other belief systems different than yours?

    Yes, more than No _____ No, more than Yes_____

16. Are you interested in trying out new techniques, like meditation, to expand your consciousness?

    Yes, more than No _____ No, more than Yes _____

17. Do you have a growing desire to inquire more deeply into the nature of the self?

    Yes, more than No _____ No, more than Yes _____

18. Are you engaged in a regular practice of meditation?

    Yes, more than No _____ No, more than Yes _____

19. Are you working with a counselor who is helping you heal negative thoughts and emotions blocking your inward journey?

    Yes, more than No _____ No, more than Yes_____

20. Has your desire for inner exploration become more a priority than road trips or vacations?

    Yes, more than No _____ No, more than Yes _____

21. Do you wish to learn how to navigate both the inner and outer worlds equally?

    Yes, more than No _____   No, more than Yes _____

22. Have you acquired a longing to make complete sense of human existence, in both its material and spiritual aspects?

    Yes, more than No _____   No, more than Yes _____

23. Do you want to know how to more fully be in the world from the meaningful and purposeful point of view of your soul?

    Yes, more than No _____   No, more than Yes _____

24. Are you engaged in practices that strengthen the senses of your soul and enable you to connect more with your higher intelligence?

    Yes, more than No _____   No, more than Yes _____

25. Do you feel that you are becoming better equipped to continue your soul's journey in a physical form?

    Yes, more than No _____   No, more than Yes _____

The questions above are divided into five sequences:

- Dweller (1–5)
- Questioner (6–10)
- Wanderer (11–15)
- Aspirant (16–20)
- Wayfarer (21–25)

If you answer "yes" to at least three questions in any of the five sequences, this will be an indicator of your seeker stage profile. Do not worry if you see parts of yourself in more than one stage. Your consciousness is always making inroads to further expansion.

Now that you have taken a look at how far you may have already come on the seeker's way of soul, in soul journey 2 is a glimpse of what lies ahead for you. This exercise will help to activate your soul's sense of sight. Learning to visualize the possible, when the possible is rooted in truth, invigorates the actual and puts your soul on its course. Envisioning is a practice of truth, of unfolding what is already in seed form and finding a clear pathway to the soul's ultimate fruition.

SOUL JOURNEY 2
Soul Vision

MEDITATION

Go to a favorite spot where you can enjoy a moment of solitude. Close your eyes. Enter your breathing room. Take two strong breaths, connecting immediately your mind with your body. Breathe naturally from that deep place in your stomach. Feel the rise and fall of your breath as you inhale and exhale.

Let your thoughts come and go like waves lapping against the bow of a boat. Some of them might be crashing against the rocks. It doesn't matter. Just turn on the inner light of your being.

AWAKENING EXERCISE

Imagine yourself on a magnificent ship. You are sailing over rolling waves toward a mysterious and alluring shore you can hardly make out in the distance.

You look behind you and there is only ocean. You say to yourself, I have become a seeker: a sincere questioner and a bright-eyed wanderer, a devoted aspirant of the soul, about to uncover the secret of the higher self and, as well, the secrets of the universe.

Open your eyes. Look out upon your world with the strong heart of a wayfarer, eager to learn how to navigate the inner and outer seas of life, ever shifting. Let your soul say a big yes to becoming a great force in and for the world.

As you move through your day today, stay open for a brand new chapter of your story waiting to be written.

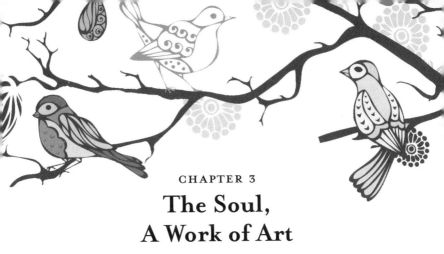

CHAPTER 3

The Soul, A Work of Art

IF YOU HAVEN'T ALREADY, one day you will come to the startling realization that your soul is a grand work of art in the making. Your soul is the great artist of you. Becoming your soul is a moment by moment practice, a way of being. Whenever you become your soul, you are creating your authentic self. This is true individuality.

When you root your potentials in the truth of who you are, you avoid taking side trips into fantasy. Although fantasy surely has its place in freeing the limited mind from its tendency to get stuck in ruts, visualizing potential is different.

Envision yourself as a work of art, an ongoing creation in process. When you embrace the path of identifying with your soul's potential, you will no longer be afraid to fail. Failure becomes uninteresting. Like a musician in the middle of a learned piece of music, a mistake often morphs into welcomed improvisations. Some of the most significant inventions have emerged as a consequence of a mistake suddenly turned into a groundbreaking surprise.

The more you identify with the creative dimension of your soul, the less you need to impress others. Your focus is more on the reasons of why you are here and why you have taken a physical form. Why did your soul choose this earth experience? What is your soul meant to accomplish? Your soul may have come to partake in a particular career path, or the path of marriage and children. Your soul may have come to engineer the material forms of earth, to build and furnish a home, or to grow plants and flowers. Your soul may have come here to enjoy the play of sex in a body; to master a sport; or to express yourself through the art forms of music, dance, painting, sculpture, or acting.

Your soul will most always have multiple purposes. But your soul will also have an overarching purpose for its sojourn through the material world. There is a singular, overriding purpose of your soul. Enjoy the search to find it.

The work of art a seeker wishes to become is not the construction of a powerful and influential self as seen by the many. The genuine work of art is often hidden away from public view and often not understood by the public eye. Only the seeker awakened to their soul understands the significance of this.

Breaking with convention for the sake of shock value is the work of a self-based artist. If a person's life should break away from the crowd and be seen in its soulful singularity, it will be the consequence of an authentic life lived. An enduring sense of joyful aim can scarcely become a reality unless one is focused on one's own genuine path. This path can only be forged by your soul.

In soul journey 3, you are invited to deepen this important and basic practice of creating yourself. When you install affirmations into your visualization practice, you learn how to both ground the imaginal in the actual and inspire the actual through the imaginal. Experience how the portrait of your soul that is already being sketched comes to life through the twofold power of visualization and affirmation.

SOUL JOURNEY 3
Creating Soul

MEDITATION

After locating a calming space, get in a comfortable sitting position. Close your eyes and enter your breathing room within.

Follow the natural flow of your breath with focused awareness. Witness the movie reel of your thoughts. Know that anything that may roll in and out of view is outside of you. Pay little attention to this. These thoughts are not you. Centered in your soul, you are protected by who you really are. Continue to follow your breath with your awareness for five minutes.

Awakening Exercise

As you do this breath work, reflect on two episodes of your life up to now: a win and then a loss. These are examples of your soul's epic adventure from the viewpoint of your material mind. Actually, all of your life's outcomes constitute merely the outer layer of something deeper at work wishing to be born.

Even though you may only see a humble sketch of it, the contour of your soul is now taking shape. You are also beginning to see the contour of other souls coming into recognition of their own splendid form. As your soul becomes more enfleshed and materializes in the here and now, you see your soul as who you really are.

Read the following words of affirmation out loud or in silence: I am becoming a work of art that brings to me and to the world not sadness, but joy.

CHAPTER 4
Creative Seeing

WITH SOUL SIGHT, YOU don't have to filter everything through your opinions and belief systems anymore. You live with more clarity and calm. Your brain produces more life-enhancing chemicals.

As you identify more with your higher mind, you will look upon the world as a school of multiple systems, each having their own relevance.

In contrast, your lower mind is nearsighted and convinces you that your view of reality should be everyone else's. Your lower mind has a long checklist of thoughts, feelings, and behaviors that are "right" and "wrong." It takes a lot of energy to defend a singular view of the world.

Composed of beginner, intermediate, and advanced classes, the school of the soul uses an experimental trial and error method that tests the benefit of what you hold to be true. The wisdom gained from a life fully lived is fathomless in comparison to a life half-lived from a small-minded place of narrowness and fear.

A limiting perspective is any thought, concept, doctrine, or worldview that draws a hard boundary around your mind. Visualize for a moment a closed circle or a box. Place your worldview inside it, and you will immediately get what I am saying.

A limiting perspective can be broadened and deepened by activating the mind of the soul. To accomplish this, all you have to do is cultivate an internal attitude of openness. Openness relaxes your material mind, enabling you to see any issue from a number of sides.

Over time, the practice of shifting awareness from a narrow and anxious mind to an open and relaxed one provides a healthy sense of internal spaciousness. Spaciousness accommodates the soul's natural tendency to entertain and, ultimately, benefit from the understanding of multiple views.

I recall a powerful soul education experience as an undergraduate in philosophy. Students often engaged one another in debate forums in the cafeteria over coffee. There were many lively discussions between representatives of differing schools of thought.

On this particular day, one of my philosophy professors asked me to stay after class. Without saying a word, he proceeded to draw a number of circles on the chalkboard.

He inscribed the name of a philosophical school in each of the circles. After doing so he turned to me and asked, "Put a check next to the one you think is the true philosophy." Of course, without hesitation I checked my preference. He smiled and said, "You are right!"

Just as I was about to gloat with intellectual satisfaction, the professor put a check next to every one of the remaining circles and said to me, "Every one of these schools of thought are correct," he said. "Each has followed the logic of an undergirding premise to its end. Yet, all of these philosophies are closed circles and as such, are closed systems."

After he gave me a minute to gather myself, the professor concluded, "You will need to ask yourself whether you will ever be satisfied with a closed system. Closed systems tend to create closed minds. That is all."

The results of that teaching moment that occurred after the class session had ended didn't happen in a flash. It took a number of years before this life lesson really sank in, opening me up to the vastness of the mind.

In soul journey 4, you will learn how to expand your soul's sense of sight through an alert relaxation of the mind. This particular exercise is designed to lessen any anxiety you might feel around the concept of open systems thinking. Relaxing the mind also helps to address any negative judgments you may have around the ideas of others with whom you may strongly disagree.

SOUL JOURNEY 4
Relaxing the Mind

MEDITATION

Take your place in a spot where you can enter a meditative spirit of presence. In this space of inner quiet, close your eyes, and let your breathing room come to life.

Tune in with your mind to the natural cadence of your breath. Let your mind flow as it attaches to every nuance of each inhaled and exhaled breath.

As thoughts arise to pull your awareness away from your breathing rhythm, return to the practice of attaching your mind to your breath.

Attentive breathing relaxes your mind and creates spaciousness within you. Feel into this spaciousness. Feel more relaxed in this attentive breathing, as fleeting thoughts lose their power to distract and unsettle you. Practice this for a few minutes or whatever time frame feels comfortable.

AWAKENING EXERCISE

Think of a core belief or an idea that you are invested in or an opinion you have on a certain matter. When you find one, explore it, and ask yourself: "Why is this so important to me?" Acknowledge why you might need this belief, idea, or opinion in your life.

Imagine you're walking into a colorful shop of gifts and you see a big box lying upon a shelf. You take the box down and open its cover. Inside, you find a smaller box and inside that one an even smaller one, and so on, until you come to the tiniest box.

Now go to the big one again and see that it is inside the box of the shop. And the shop is inside the box of the town, and the town is inside the box of the state, and a country, and the earth is within the box of the solar system, and within it other universes ... and on and on it goes.

Zoom back into the box that is your material mind and body. Slowly open your eyes and look around you. Feel the coziness of the box of your room. Ease into the serene spaciousness of your soul. See the world around you with more clarity and calm, now that you have relaxed your mind and thereby expanded your soul's sense of sight.

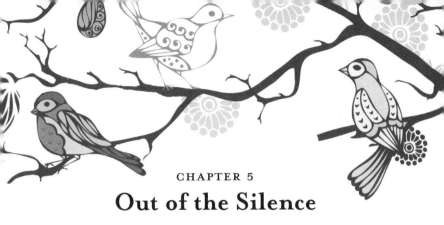

CHAPTER 5
Out of the Silence

AN EFFECTIVE WAY TO cultivate a creative mind is to establish a regular routine of meditation. I have chosen for this book the simple but powerful method of gently attaching your awareness to your breath. This practice enlivens your breathing with the energy of higher consciousness.

Integral to this technique is the incorporation of visualization. Visualization engages the imaginative dimension of mind and aids in dissolving obsessive and negative thinking.

There are many layers of meaning around the word "meditation." All of us have experienced meditation in some form or another. For instance, thinking over a matter of importance for a length of time is the most common use of the term.

At a deeper level, meditation is the receptive and penetrating stillness of awareness. Watch how busy your material mind is. This is your lower intelligence, the thinker. It is never still for a moment unless sunk in the waters of sleep. Now connect with this silent witness within you, the seer within your core. This is your higher intelligence, the knower. This is your soul.

The knower inside of you is independent of your lower intelligence. From the vantage point of your higher intelligence, the chaotic world in which you live becomes easier to deal with and even shrinks in size.

You are developing a growing awareness of the limitless dimension of consciousness within you. You are learning to envision with your expanded soul sight the quality of spaciousness within you. Every thought arises from and vanishes into inner spaciousness.

In ancient schools of spiritual education, spans of silence were considered essential to learning deep truths. It has been said that the ancient Greek mathematician and mystic Pythagoras assigned to his students several years of periodic silence before introducing them to the deeper mysteries of the soul.

A meditative mind expands not only the soul's sense of sight but also the soul's sense of hearing. During my first days as a novice, living in a Benedictine monastery, I discovered an extraordinary silence that exists at the bottom of the well of sound. It wasn't the silence of not speaking. It was rather the silence of listening, of waiting upon the whispering voice of my soul in the breeze. It was the silence in the call of the mourning dove and the silence within the loon's haunting echo passing over the trees. It was the silence in the quivering wings of bees and within the cracking ice of frozen lakes.

If you have ever been lulled or carried away for a moment by the song of the wind, the pattering of the rain, the lap of the ocean wave, or the call of bird, you have experienced, ever so briefly, the silence of listening.

In your own way, you have felt the silence within the hum beneath all of these sounds. Your soul hears every nuance, every reverberation. This is the great rhythm, the heartbeat of the earth that echoes to the heavens.

Meditation is a way of seeing into the invisible and hearing into the silence, from a place of deep, inner listening. Listening from our soul gives us an ability to feel the vibration within the material world of objects and within all living things. When soul hearing matures, it has been said that one can hear celestial music.

The struck chord of the harps of angels is a metaphor for something far greater. The renderings of Bach, Beethoven, and the Indian ragas are faint echoes of something more magnificent. The collective soul mind knows universally the sounds that create joy and those that create sadness.

There are two distinct realms that coexist in the physical world: the lower realm of material mind and the higher realm of soul mind. These realms are not meant to be separate but are designed to flow into one another, inform and enrich one another.

Meditation is a way of seeing and hearing in a refined way with our physical eyes and ears, though from the profoundly perceptive senses of our soul. That is why meditation is more than just a way of thinking. Meditation is a way of being.

In soul journey 5, you will activate your soul's sense of hearing. This exercise will also help to bring any discordant thoughts and feelings that disturb the mind into harmony.

SOUL JOURNEY 5
Hearing with Soul

MEDITATION

Sit quietly with your eyes closed in a fitting space. Enter your breathing room and imagine you are sitting there. Follow the natural flow of your breath. Be gentle with your inner gaze and let your thoughts—like clouds—cross the horizon of your mind and watch them as they linger or float past, moving in and out of view.

Accept any and all external sounds that may come into your hearing range. Listen to the rhythms of what you hear with an attitude of total receptivity. Let your being become spacious enough to include noise, allowing all vibrations in your outer space to pass through you. Listen without effort. Be soft of hearing and take in a cup of that silence, the pauses between the sounds.

Do this for five breath cycles.

Awakening Exercise

As you continue your breath work, stay open, receptive, and spacious. You may sense a deeper vibration that underlies all the sounds around you, a continuous hum on the low end and a high-pitched signal on the high end. Don't worry if you do not.

Just know the song of the universe is always playing and sometimes you may even hear a faint echo. Feel now that you are in the flow, in the great rhythm of life. Imagine that your heartbeat and breath are in sync with this great rhythm, the heartbeat and breath of the universe.

Open your eyes and stay attentive to your soul's hearing every sound around you, layered and rich in texture. This is the sound and silence of light. Take all of this in as you would a favorite piece of music. Whether you are aware or not, know that your soul's sense of hearing is now permanently activated. Return to this exercise whenever you wish to strengthen this mode of soul perception.

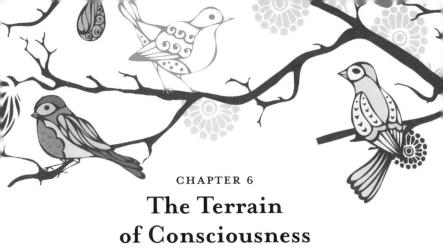

CHAPTER 6

The Terrain
of Consciousness

THE CONSCIOUS PATH OF making soul sense accelerates when you answer the call of that tug from within, from that higher intelligence that is your soul. Now that key senses of your soul have been activated and you are cultivating a meditative and creative mind, it will be important to acquire a basic map of the terrain of consciousness.

There are several layers of awareness. You mastered the first three naturally not long after you were born, when you became a dweller on the earth.

The first layer is the sleep state, when your lower mind merges with the unconscious. Your once active body and mind unplug from daily responsibilities and you can re-energize through rest.

The second layer is your lower mind's dream state within sleep. Here the realm of your imagination plays out actively within your dreams. Your dreams are the place where wish fulfillments are often enacted. Sometimes fragmented and opposing parts of yourself with numerous masks and faces will appear on the stage of your dreams.

Taking on a life and drama of their own, learning ways to integrate your dreams into your life will give you a measure of inner peace. Don't concern yourself if you don't remember most of your dreams. The ones you need to decipher will get your attention if they need to.

The third layer of awareness is your lower mind's waking state. Your lower mind organizes received data and sees everything in dualities—subject/object, teacher/student, man/woman, child/adult, good/evil, light/dark, and so on.

Most of us spend our lives in dweller, questioner, or wanderer consciousness. All three of these seeker states remain within the range of the three layers of the sleep, dream, and waking realms.

The exercises is in this book assist you in becoming familiar with the fourth layer of consciousness. This is where the pull into relaxed and alert inwardness actually happens. It is here where you are initiated into the aspirant and wayfarer paths. Over a period of time, any practice of attaching your awareness to the movement of your breath will establish the preconditions for awakening to your essence as soul.

If you persist in your inner practices, you may arrive at the fifth layer of consciousness, identifying with your soul as the subject, witness, and navigator of your physical body and lower mind. Your higher mind interacts with all things in the material world from a place of empathy and freedom. At the fifth layer of consciousness, you receive glimpses and a felt sense of the interrelated web of energy that connects you to all things. You have become a seasoned wayfarer.

When the senses of the soul are fully operative, one may have a felt experience of the interconnectedness between all things. This is the true meaning of the mystical life.

The sixth layer of consciousness is unveiled to you after you learn to maintain more elongated periods of connective consciousness while experiencing daily life. At the sixth layer you see and/or feel an intimate connection to every material thing, though in its less dense form, as energy.

At some point in the long journey of the soul, all of us will arrive at the seventh layer of awareness. When this happens, your higher intelligence (or soul) unites with infinite intelligence (or the beyond soul) while fully awake. When the advanced seeker is established in this state without a pause or a break, they become completely soul-realized while in a physical body.

A fully actualized human being has attained Buddha or Christ consciousness. This level of awareness is a continuous state of infinite being (sat), infinite consciousness (chit), and infinite bliss (ananda), satchitananda in the Sanskrit. The goal of every soul that comes into the world is to actualize sat chit ananda. In fact, right now, your soul is infinite being, infinite consciousness, and infinite bliss, only in its "becoming" and partially realized state.

Let's hike back down the mountain a few steps to the fourth layer of consciousness, where the seeker has been initiated into the path of the aspirant. Once we have discovered that our meditative mind has always been our real mind and that our soul has always been our real self, we are on the trail toward enlightenment. This is the path of the aspirant. The aspirant is on the royal road of wakefulness.

If you have already taken in to some degree the gist of the previous chapters, you have answered the call to the aspirant's journey of inwardness. That felt pull in consciousness to travel inward and upward into your essence is a divine gravity, a call to return home to the fertile soil of your soul.

In soul journey 6, your consciousness is drawn to that fertile soil, where the seed of the soul has been planted, nurtured, and set to flower. Through this exercise you can establish the preconditions for an experience of that felt pull within. The phenomenon of divine gravity is actually the growth of your soul happening now within your body, your heart, and your mind. Return often to this exercise whenever you need to be recharged with energy for the wonderful work of growing your soul in the material world.

SOUL JOURNEY 6
Divine Gravity

MEDITATION

After you have entered your breathing room within, sit comfortably, with your eyes closed. With your awareness, follow the natural flow of your breath. Feel the cool air as you inhale through your nose, and the warm air as you exhale through your nose. Rest your tongue flat upon the roof of your mouth without forcing anything. This will enable a good portion of air to easily pass through your nostrils.

As you inhale, relax your stomach, allowing it to extend as your diaphragm descends. As you exhale, your stomach will naturally recede as your diaphragm rises. Relax into the pause after each exhale, sensing the soft pull into inwardness.

I invite you to do this for five minutes and then proceed to the awakening exercise.

Awakening Exercise

Continuing the meditation, take a few seconds to hear the sounds of everything around you, but soften the intensity of what you hear in the following way:

Let any external or internal sounds and the silence between them simply come and go through you like a mild breeze lifting the branches of a strong and well-rooted tree.

Now imagine a gentle rain falling upon you. Breathe in every molecule from above into every part of your body, from your head all the way down to your toes. Feel the energy from beneath you and from above. Feel this divine gravity coaxing you ever inward and upward, and imagine your soul unfolding its buds that one day will flower.

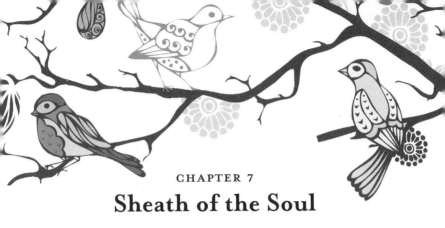

CHAPTER 7

Sheath of the Soul

THE PHYSICAL BODY OF the soul is its sheath, and as such, an intimate part of the soul's life. Every living thing, including the earth itself, is a holy sheath, glistening with soul.

Our bodies depend upon all that lives and blossoms within the soil and in the water. We partake of the sheaths of soul that fly across the skies of the earth. Every moment of our waking hours is an opportunity to enter the vibrant energy of life with the awareness that we are here to deepen the soul's embodiment.

Like a sail fully extended, the sheath of your soul needs to catch the wind in its folds. Life is waiting to take you on a new adventure, forever opening to unknown vistas and grander webs of connection.

It is only through the body that your soul can experience life in all of its manifold forms to its utmost. Your body already knows this. It is your material mind that gets in the way. You have to reconnect with your soul mind, already woven into your body to counteract this problem.

There are many kinds of "intelligences" that make up a human being that warrant further evaluation. In addition to the mental IQ, there are emotional and spiritual degrees of comprehension. The intelligence of the embodied soul needs to be figured into the mix when assessing a human being's complex modes of knowing.

We have been exploring the multiple senses of the soul that, when cultivated, will give us heightened perception. There is a dormant intelligence within the fibers of the body that waits to be wired with soul. Once you give to your material body the soul consciousness it most desires, you will have more energy than you know what to deal with.

When you realize that the body's purpose is to manifest soul in the material world, your ideas about health care, including the maintenance and strengthening of the body, will shift into a higher gear. Your soul is the one, continuous entity that has been with you since your eyes first looked into a mirror. That luminous entity has been with your body, through all its hairstyles, clothes of fashion, injuries, scars, and signs of age.

Your real "I" has always been the one looking back at the different material versions of "you" throughout your life. If there is any proof for the plausibility of reincarnation it is in this one fact: that the continuity of the subject, the experiencer, the soul, has been, is, and always will be, you.

But you must find this out for yourself, not once or twice, but as many times as you can until your true identity becomes second nature to you. You are an embodied soul. This is who you are.

As you proceed to soul journey 7 bring the awareness of embodiment with you. You will be guided to awaken your body with the warm consciousness of your soul. Through this exercise you can feel the healing effects of soul consciousness as it fills your body with life.

SOUL JOURNEY 7
Awaken Your Body

MEDITATION

Find a comfortable spot as free of noise as possible and get situated. Close your eyes. Enter your breathing room within and take your seat there. Bring your awareness to the rise and fall of your breath. Let your breath do what it wants to. The breath-as-spirit desires to manifest its nature in and through your body.

Let warm consciousness infuse your body, the sheath of your soul. Catch yourself whenever you get swept away by schemas, tapes of desire produced by your material mind. Return to the simple breathing of the life force in your body. Do this for two minutes or more.

Awakening Exercise

Give yourself the following affirmations with an open heart:

I open further into soul embodiment, to the physicality of my soul and how it enlivens and empowers my body.

As I shift my awareness from my thoughts to my breath-as-spirit I feel the subtleties and healing power of my soul.

Breathing life into my body, I bring kind awareness to any particular place in need of loving attention.

Today, I will memorize by heart the following affirmation: I do all I can to nurture my body because it is the flesh of my soul.

CHAPTER 8
Soul Music

ATTUNEMENT DESCRIBES THE SOUL'S sense of inner pitch, tone, and vibration. Similar to the way our ears filter out pleasant from disturbing sounds, the soul is attracted to coherence, to harmony within the self, with others, and with all living things.

Tuning in and tuning out is something the lower intelligence most often does without knowing it. Attunement, however, is the norm for our higher intelligence. When we talk about being "on the same wavelength" with another person, this rapport between minds is actually a blend of thought and feeling energies. We create a more cheerful atmosphere and a shared lightness of being when we are in mental harmony with another.

Soul sensitive persons pick up the positive or negative tones of voices in conversation. When harmony between others is absent, the energy of opposing wavelengths can be felt, even in the thickened air of silence.

Emotions we associate with mental and emotional disharmony are sluggishness, apathy, fear, sorrow, distrust, and anger. Discordant wavelengths drain us of energy and disconnect us from the higher-frequency emotions of kindness and empathy.

One of the reasons the soul is here with others in the material world is to learn how and in what measure to give, receive, deflect, neutralize, or harmonize energy. For instance, meeting chaotic or unwholesome energy with nonjudgmental fearlessness is an effective neutralizer.

Once you become soul conscious, you are always free to change your internal state of mind. Learn to be accountable to your own soul. A toxic mental environment is contagious. A protective guard is to return to your home base practice, of breathing into your core with kind awareness.

You can also incorporate a mantra into your breath practice as a daily hygiene of soul. A word or vowel mantra spoken, sung, or taken into the heart and mind silently is probably the most ancient method of affirmation. Sound contains energy. A well-formed one can shift you from a lower to a higher vibrational frequency.

The soul's hearing sense can be strengthened through the use of vocal "toning" (or chanting). The toning of an ancient vowel sound, word, or phrase helps to bring the soul into accord with the body and mind like a tuning fork.

Traditionally, a mantra was based on the vowel system of an ancient vocalized language that conveyed the vibrational sounds of creation (for example, the Sanskrit AUM or OM. Mantras have been known to accelerate awareness and to activate sublime qualities within the soul's physical body, such as clarity of speech or internal calm).

Primal mantras, such as ah, mah, dah, lah, and tah are contained in the rudiments of speech in every language. Ah expresses the first moments when a soul (atma in the Sanskrit) enters its body out of the eternal silence. Ah expresses the embodied soul's wonderment, pleasure, relief, and serenity before actual words are formed. Mah expresses the safety, comfort and intimacy between the soul, its mother, and all of nature. Dah expresses the soul's connection to the outside world, the need for exploration, and the soul's relationship with all things that symbolize the father world. Lah expresses the soul's natural inclination to the music and rhythm of life. Tah expresses action and doing and is associated with the soul's first handling of physical objects and eventual skill in navigating the material world. Language begins as an expression of the soul's initial stages of life in a body.

As long as it conveys a positive charge to the mind, an effective affirmation can also be acquired from a modern language. It is best to not get too tied up in thinking about what a vowel, word, or phrase means while in meditation. Incorporating a positive energy word into your attentive breathing technique attunes your mind not to the word's derived meaning but to the energy that word conveys.

An advanced teacher may impart to a student a mantra intended for a specific purpose. Many years ago I received such a mantra and benefited greatly from it. Over the years I have found that any word or phrase of affirmation can assist your soul-centering practice, as long as it holds a positive charge for you.

I have also found that a mantra does not have to be used with every breath but can be employed as a tethering mechanism to call you back to your center whenever you get distracted.

Over time, an effective mantric affirmation produces positive thought forms that can erase negative ones. Most thought forms are impressions of energy projected to you from the outside. We accept impressions into our mental force field from others as well as from the environment around us all the time.

Those unaware are susceptible to taking in negative thought forms from other unconscious souls as well as negative residue from places that have been infected with toxic thoughts, words, or deeds.

Nothing works more swiftly to erase negativity than the powerful force of intelligent light. The soul is intelligent light, a unique conduit of energy, your own truest existence traveling through time. All of us are here to learn how to take responsibility for aligning our energy with the life force within and around us.

With practice you can learn to attune yourself to the current of that luminous being within you. Feel this current. Listen to it. Hear the music of its vibration. In turn, your soul will radiate its energy through the instrument of your body, like the sun's song of light through the trunks of trees. The light of your soul understands and likens itself to that heavenly glow that emanates from and radiates within all living things.

In soul journey 8, we will use the five ancient mantras —ah, mah, dah, la, and tah—to help recharge your soul's hearing sense. These mantras can be used often as tools for attunement.

SOUL JOURNEY 8
Attunement

MEDITATION

Find a fitting physical space where you can sit quietly and close your eyes. Enter your breathing room within. Take two strong breaths, connecting your awareness with your body to give you a sense of immediate presence. Now inhale into and exhale from that deep place in your core. Accept wherever you happen to be mentally and energetically—up or down—in your spirit.

Regardless of the time of day, let your thoughts and feelings come and go like clouds across the sky. Should they linger, be patient with them. Give your thoughts the warmth of affection and the light of gentle awareness without clinging to them because you are not your thoughts. You are the energy of pure, flowing consciousness. Attune to this spiritual truth as you breathe in this knowledge. Experience it. Do this for several minutes.

Awakening Exercise

Feel your self connect with the harmonizing energy of your soul. Sound out each of the ancient mantras: ah, mah, dah, lah, and tah. Take into your being the power and wonder that each of these mantras convey.

Sense now the innate intelligence of your body, mind, and soul blending into one chord, heightening the hearing sense of your soul.

Allow the buoyant energy of attunement to raise your spirits. Rest for a moment in the knowledge that your essence is a flower of golden light with these five petals that accord with the splendor and music of earth. As you go about your day, quietly emanate appreciation for the music of creation you once knew as a child and that you have now rediscovered. A smile from your soul will uplift the world around you without a word ever spoken.

CHAPTER 9
The Soul on Earth

THE SOUL KNOWS HOW to shift from the doing mode of action to the being mode of action because this is its natural embodied state. Think of a huge oak tree or sequoia. Think of any tree with thick bark and deep roots and this will give you an idea of the power of your enfleshed soul. When you learn to enter into the mystery of being, your soul's embodied nature will reveal itself to you. Being is a teacher that instructs and reveals the essence of human nature.

All soul action has its origin in being, not in thinking. In soul action there is integrity between being and doing. The soul acts according to the earth's nature. The earth's nature is being. The soul knows this and gently urges the material mind to listen and observe the way of the earth, the way of being.

When we observe an animal either in the wild or a creature friend of ours, we witness the complete identity between being and doing, nature and its soulful action. Soulful action gently and assertively streams out of the tranquil center where being dwells.

Being is the source of any wise thought, word, or deed. Rooted in being, the soul consults the wisdom within the heart. The soul knows that a period of inner silence is required before offering an answer to an important question. Inner silence is quietude. Quietude is the ocean bed and earthen bed of being. Out of this fecund stillness, the cells and seeds of all life burst into manifold form and movement.

Every possible expression of goodness, beauty, and truth emerges from being, just as the varying forms of leaf, flower and fruit arise from the roots of the seedling embedded in the fertile earth. And just as a magnificent tree or exquisite flower can evoke a sense of awe, when you ground yourself in the soil of the soul and behold the wonder of being, yet another powerful inner sense is suddenly aroused: Awe.

Awe is the profound feeling of wonder that came naturally to you when you were a child and is likely related to the infant's natural mantric (or openmouthed) sound, "ah." If you have lost or misplaced your sense of awe, it can dawn once again when you connect with your soul. Then you will see the world once again through the eyes of being.

Over time, the sense of awe produces a natural humility and reverence for our walk upon this sacred earth. Beware of the eraser of awe within your mind, that inner cynic that may try to convince you that you are an unworthy stone, undeserving and without significance, lost in a whirling universe of heartless atoms. Your soul, of course, knows that none of this is true.

Wonder will lead you on a path of soulful seeing, touching, smelling, tasting, and hearing. Sit for a while under this vast canopy of tree, mountain, sky, and star with the expansive sense of amazement, and you will always know what to do.

In soul journey 9, you are led into being, into the nature of the enfleshed soul, into the eternal ground it shares with the nature of the earth. This stress-reducing exercise will help you get out of the thinking mode of your material mind and into the being mode of your soul mind.

SOUL JOURNEY 9
Start with Being

MEDITATION

Find a shelter for a period of brief solitude. Sit comfortably. Close your eyes and enter the breathing room within you. Take two strong breaths, enough to feel your chest expand. This will bring your mind and body together in a synchrony of presence.

Imagine a column of energy moving through the center of your body, starting from the top of your head and descending downward to your feet. As you inhale, using your awareness as a pulley, bring that energy downward from the crown of your head to your belly. Then exhale from your belly to your feet all the way down to the ground below.

Imagine your soul as a tree of energy with roots, trunk, branches, and open leaves of light. Now take the earth energy from the ground as you inhale, breathing upward through the central column of your body to your heart center. Then exhale from your heart center all the way up and out through the crown of your head. Do this for several breaths or until you feel invigorated.

Awakening Exercise

Bring the image of yourself as a sitting, standing, and walking tree into your mind. Bask in the goodness, beauty, and truth of the reality of your soul that is rooted in being. Feel the grandeur of yourself as an individual soul on this earth.

Today, as you engage with the chaos of the world, the one important ACT of your soul today is to Accept, Center, and Trust.

Accept whatever comes.

Center your self in being.

Trust and let being direct you to all doing.

Sit, stand, and walk from a sense of being and open another sense of your soul. Open up to awe. Be in awe. Be awe.

CHAPTER 10

The Soul in Time

HAVE YOU EVER GOTTEN up out of bed in the morning to prepare your coffee or tea, or pour yourself some juice or water, and suddenly became conscious that it was just another repeat, another Groundhog Day?

This awareness of the mundane routines of repetition is actually the beginning of true wakefulness. When we have the sense that the passage of time in blocks of minutes and hours is unreal, we are waking up to soul.

The lower mind is programmed. It runs a tape of patterns and habits without thinking about them. The lower mind is asleep. It doesn't know how to find the extraordinary within the ordinary or the new within the old. Only the higher mind can accomplish this.

Catch yourself when you find that you are bored and distract yourself by engaging in superficial activity. Boredom is actually anxiety in disguise. Boredom is emptiness. When you are surfing the internet or clicking the remote for the next channel, choose instead to sit with your boredom. Sit with your emptiness for a minute.

Consciously connect with your essence as a clear, flowing stream of energy moving up from the earth and down from the sky into your body and mind. You will discover that there is aliveness within you that coexists both in time and outside of time. There is a reason for this.

Time and material reality provide the slowing down of experience so that we can learn what notes we are to play on the instrument of our physical body in the symphonic orchestra of the universe. To learn a musical instrument, you have to familiarize yourself with it. You have to slowly train your hands and your ears to feel the cadence and subtleties of the notes as you form and sound the various chords.

Music is a good example of the felt experience of timelessness within time. Whenever we are playing, singing, or hearing a song, we experience something ethereal yet tactile suddenly breaking through the world of time. We are carried away by rhythm and melody. That's because a musical piece has its own time signature, having nothing to do with the hour and minute hands on a clock.

Similarly, since your true essence is the existence of your soul, even though you are in a body subject to time, your soul is who and what you are, regardless of the passage of seconds, minutes, hours, days, weeks, months, and years. Your soul is your individualized consciousness and your body is your soul's vehicle traveling through time.

You may revisit a book you have read long ago. If that book is timeless and deep, it will speak to your soul as if those words were an intimate part of your own journey, now unfolding. Time periods or styles of fashion and taste don't matter to the life of the soul because for the soul there is no time, save the timeless time of being and being's becoming.

Being embraces time and every moment that has ever passed and every moment that will come. What is most important is this stream of moments that your mind, body, heart, and soul are experiencing right now. You were meant to partake of earth's splendor and to bask in the light of being that awaits every soul like a dearest friend.

In soul journey 10, you are led into a practice of how to return to being in daily life by becoming aware of the strong pull of your thoughts that take you out of presence.

SOUL JOURNEY 10
The Eternal Moment of Being

MEDITATION

Find a fitting physical space to sit comfortably and quietly in a low-lit room. Close your eyes and enter your breathing room within. Take two strong breaths expanding your chest, and then exhale with some force. This will help your mind connect with your body.

Breathe naturally, allowing all sounds around you to come and go. Bring your awareness to the sensations in your body. Notice where there may be knots of energy in your back, shoulders, neck, and jaw. Gently press into any sensitive area with your fingers.

Give yourself caring touch by bringing your attention to a specific place in your body that might present stiffness, burning, or any discomfort. There may be a part of your body that is totally numb. Take a deep breath and breathe into one of these areas; massage it slowly and as deeply as you can tolerate.

Awakening Exercise

Open your eyes and look out into your world with the presence of sensation, aware that it is only your body—including your brain—that is traveling through time and subject to its laws.

Recall the three dimensions of time: chronological (clock time), psychological (material mind time), and ontological (soul mind time); notice what dimension of time you find yourself dwelling in most often.

Practice being present to the eternal moment of being—to the timeless time of your soul—all day today.

Stay aware of whatever you happen to be doing—whatever it may be—without analysis other than noting the following: Is this thought I'm having pleasant or unpleasant? Is this about the past or about the future?

After noting where you are in your thoughts, return and be in the now.

Return ... return ... return to the timeless now that always is.

PART TWO
Strengthening Soul in the Material World

YOU HAVE ANSWERED THE call to the inward journey to increase your consciousness and grow in spiritual knowledge. You are learning how to take responsibility for your own energy. Now it is time to harness, channel, and harmonize this energy, which is the elixir of the soul.

To accomplish this requires an inventory of your soul's resources. In this way you will gain more experiential knowledge to fortify the soul on its chosen path. New thresholds, new worlds, always farther than the soul can see, await the aspirant and wayfarer.

Throughout the centuries, masters of the inward journey have provided a rich variety of practices, called "yogas," for the purpose of strengthening the soul for its journey through the material world.

There are a number of ways one may extrapolate on the meaning of yoga. The word itself comes from the Sanskrit *yuj* meaning to "yoke" or "to unify." The yogas help to unify body-force with mind-force and mind-force with soul-force, all to bring equanimity rather than polarization to the mind.

The yogas aid in the "bringing together of forces" within the self for the purpose of experiencing life to its fullest. The yogas also teach us how to bring the high energy of the soul's senses into the body's senses to inform and enliven them.

The soul mind is hardwired for this process. The senses of the soul are receptors that enhance communication between the nonphysical soul and its physical vehicle. As such, they are designed to extend in two directions, descending into the material and ascending into the spiritual.

Said another way, the soul's receptors reach into the material world through the portal of its porous sheath, its physical body. The soul's receptors also extend beyond the material world into the farther reaches of intelligence. Enhancing the soul's modes of perception allow it to tap new energy resources, thus enriching the soul's ability to experience more fully the material world.

The following chapters present seven yogas, pathways to wholeness. Each of the yogas will teach you how to effectively channel, balance, and use the energy at your soul's reach. Look over the seven yogas outlined for you. See which one you naturally resonate with and can easily attune to. You may even wish to practice one for a while.

Though it takes a measure of commitment to follow a spiritual road for any distance, if you lose this desire for a time, do not judge yourself. A spiritual path is best when it enhances whatever career or vocation path you happen to be on.

Keep in mind that soul paths move us inward, outward, and upward. They serve to stimulate our deepest imagination of the possible and, as well, augment our ability to be more present to the actual.

The paths and their yogas are meant to affirm life and all the opportunities life presents to us. This includes all of the difficulties and challenges we will surely encounter.

Welcome to the next stage of the journey.

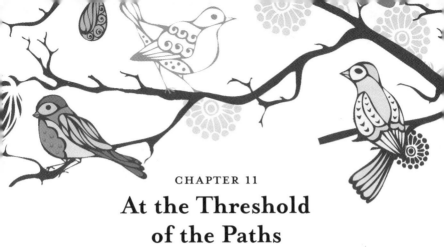

CHAPTER 11

At the Threshold
of the Paths

THERE IS AN INTELLIGENT interplay of messages sent and received between the earth, moon, and sun for the ongoing creation of life on this planet. Earth nature is a harmonious ensemble of energies that generates the four seasons of spring, summer, fall, and winter.

When we observe the natural world, we notice that force fluctuates, rising and falling according to the repeating cycles of earth nature. Earth nature possesses its own intelligence. In other words, earth nature knows exactly what it is doing.

There are seasons of the soul that mirror the seasons within nature. Similarly, the soul undergoes its own cyclic periods of growth, decay, dormancy, and renewal. Each of the soul's seasons can be of longer or shorter duration and intensity.

You must learn the inner seasons of your own soul, including its descending and ascending patterns. On the path you must learn from the season you happen to be experiencing. Recognize when you are in the middle of a winter season of inner darkness or perhaps going through a spring season of inner renewal and refreshment.

The operating system of the higher path is closer to the mechanics of nature. Nature goes into a dormant period only to emerge with new growth. Similarly, the soul knows it must lose something in order to gain something else. Like earth nature, the soul learns to take in and release, breathe in and breathe out, rise and fall, nurture and let go.

The soul knows that to let go is to practice what the native intelligence of the earth does naturally. A period of night to the soul, however long, is part of a cycle that always ends in light, in an awakening and deepening in wisdom and compassion.

Life's challenges are initiations that strengthen the soul, even though the physical body and the lower mind may sometimes feel like it is being put through the wringer. Life-to-death and death-to-life is the greater pattern that the inner seasons of the soul and the outer seasons of nature share.

What the lower mind considers to be loss, higher mind sees as boon. Something may be dying within you while something greater within you is on its way to being born.

When you finally let go, and accept that whatever's happening is a positive thing, you can turn to focus on what new deeper and broader form is beginning to take shape in you.

Nature reflects the journey of the wakeful soul. When we perceive in an empty feeling a waiting with love, in every sadness a sweet longing, and at the center of every conflict the fire of creativity, we will more fruitfully live the wisdom of the inner seasons and better comprehend the eternal wakefulness within nature.

Yoga is the intimate journey of soul-nature's bond with earth-nature. Earth reflects the essence of yoga, which is the unifying of forces. Earth mirrors the essence of soul, which contains within itself the great spiral of eternal being and eternal becoming.

In soul journey 11, reflect on the four seasons of nature, become aware of your own inner season, and allow earth nature to nurture your soul nature with its energy, wisdom, and truth. This exercise will help to increase your knowledge of the intimate relationship between your soul and the earth and deepen your understanding of others and where they happen to be in their season cycle as well.

SOUL JOURNEY 11
Seasons of the Soul

MEDITATION

Close your eyes and enter your breathing room within. Take two strong breaths to engage your mind and body, ushering you into immediate presence. Now you are here. Breathe naturally, and softly examine your interior. Scan your body and mind for moods and feelings. Are you down? Up? Neutral? Are you undergoing an inner trial or dark night of the soul? Accept it all, whatever you are feeling, without judgment or without trying to change any thought or feeling. Only bring kind consciousness to your practice and into the scene of what you see or into the feeling of what you feel.

AWAKENING EXERCISE

Picture a moon in one of its phases in your inner sky. Is it full? Waxing? Waning? Do you see a yellow harvest moon? Do you see a disc of white in a wintry sky? Allow for the particular "season of your soul" to surface to your consciousness.

Ask yourself, where am I right now in my life cycle? Accept whatever comes. Give loving attention—warmth and light—to your being, for it is always becoming. Don't fight it. Just be with the phase and mood of the moon that you see. Say to yourself, "And this, too, shall pass."

Open your eyes. Connect with a gentle gaze to the external room and to the world around you. See how everything outside of you is partaking in the light and shadow of the earth, the sun, and the moon according to the season. Your individual soul has it own days and nights, its own seasons of light and dark, and its very own harvest of purpose. As sure as the cyclical bounty of the four seasons of winter, spring, summer, and fall are already known to you, so will your destiny reveal itself to you.

Resonate and attune to your own inner season, knowing that whatever phase or cycle your soul may be in now, you are being healed by the loving consciousness of the sun, the moon, and the earth. Take this affirmation with you today:

I accept all that is dying and all that is being born within me for my highest good and for the good of all others, and for all creation.

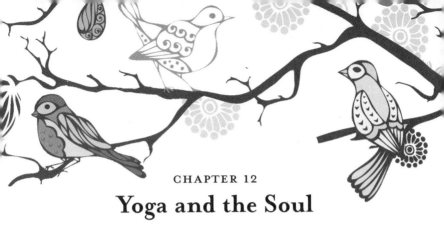

CHAPTER 12

Yoga and the Soul

FOR THE SOUL, EVERY moment of human existence is yoga. Said another way, yoga is the practice of connecting the senses of the soul with the senses of the body, the heart with the mind, matter with spirit. The soul is the great connector. The soul seeks fulfillment within its physical form because the search for wholeness and entirety is in the soul's very nature.

The origin of the yogas can be traced to the Vedas, considered the oldest teachings of Hinduism and compiled in text form around 1500 BCE. The Vedas (from the Sanskrit *veda*, meaning "revealed knowledge") covered the gamut of categories, dealing with social, philosophical, metaphysical, and mathematical themes, including practices to develop higher states of consciousness.

Each of the yogas provides a specific path and destination for the seeker. The yogas provide resources for the full life of the soul as it journeys through the material world. They offer ways for you to connect more deeply with your essence so that you may live a more vibrant life, unified in body, mind, heart, and spirit.

It is by means of the soul's higher awareness that you gain more knowledge of energy and its important role in the progress of the soul. The yogas assist the soul's intelligence in its work to harness, channel, refine, and integrate the unwieldy forces that govern the lower mind. Thoughts and feelings contain tremendous amounts of energy and tend to run rampant within the lower mind.

Whichever one you may be drawn to explore, the goal of all the yogas is to invigorate the receptors of your soul so that you may become a skilled apprentice to the truth of your infinite being. The truth of your infinite being lies within the fibers of your consciousness. The yogas energize these fibers when you exercise the body, mind, and soul together as an ensemble. In this way, your total self becomes more stable, supple, and pliant.

The more you allow your soul to permeate your mind and body, the more your bones and brain, tendons and muscles reap the benefits. Because the yogas help to connect all the parts of you, your entire nervous system is strengthened.

Your body and mind are waiting to partake of the inexhaustible energy of light and love that flows in abundance to the soul from the earth and from the heavens. This is the crux of yoga: learning how to be fully in the world of matter from the standpoint of the soul. Yoga is the moment-by-moment practice of establishing and maintaining a meaningful unity between the natural and the spiritual.

In soul journey 12, you will use breath and visualization techniques to access and take into your body the energy of earth and heaven. This exercise will serve to heighten your awareness of energy in its subtle aspects.

By understanding the integral role of yoga in strengthening your embodied soul you will be able to become more conscious, more aware, and more responsible for cultivating the powerful intelligence that lies dormant within you.

SOUL JOURNEY 12
Joining Earth Energy and Heaven Energy

MEDITATION

Find your quiet place, sit down, close your eyes, and turn your gaze within. Enter your breathing room.

Take two forceful breaths to consciously join your mind with your body and feel how this enlivens you.

Feel the energy rise from your belly as you breathe naturally from your core. Inhale upward to your head, and then exhale downward into your belly. Do this for five breath cycles.

Now, in one or more breath cycles take in earth energy. Follow this energy with your awareness as you inhale it into your feet, gently pulling it up your legs and torso and into the center of your chest as you exhale.

Next, in one or more breath cycles, inhale heaven energy into the portal at the top of your head, gently pulling it down into the center of your chest as you exhale.

Next, in one or more breath cycles, as you inhale, picture both earth energy and heaven energy enter, one ascending and the other descending, and as you exhale feel the blending of both energies as they meet at your chest center.

Awakening Exercise

Continue this practice. Simultaneously inhale earth energy up from your feet and heaven energy down from the top of your head. Sense their blending at the meeting place of your chest center.

Visualize a flower of energy at your heart center being nurtured by the influx of the two energies. Imagine this flower unfolding its petals outward and upward. Picture your soul as a flower of energy, being nurtured by the earth and heaven energies. Let the aromatic medicine of this unified energy refresh your entire being.

Feel this sense for wholeness, activated now in your chest center. Here your physical senses and the senses of your soul have met to enliven one another

Now, return your awareness to your body. Open your eyes with a soft gaze. Connect with the environment around you. Feel the light within every color you see. Sense how each color is more vivid now that your physical and soul senses have informed one another.

CHAPTER 13
Mind Yoga

THE HIGHER INTELLIGENCE WITH which you were born is your greatest asset. Growing your soul mind gives you a profound sense of mental and emotional freedom. You can acquire the ability to fully function in the material world from the vantage point of your soul through mind stretch exercises.

For example, entertain the notion that you are both finite and infinite, both flesh and spirit. This is the paradox of you. By taking a moment to concentrate on the passing of your thoughts, you realize that the subject of your awareness is an intelligence that can observe any object of thought that arises. This higher intelligence is your soul mind.

You, the thinker, are the one, continuous reality at the ground of all of your material mind's appearing and disappearing mental activity. Watch how your material mind is carried away by thoughts and emotions, unaware that you exist within a broader field of consciousness. This consciousness extends infinitely and contains all experience. Your soul mind is both within you and contains you.

The real you is the knower. The knower is your soul mind. Much of what you think to be true or false, real or unreal is actually an inherited framework that shapes your way of seeing things.

Mind yoga stretches the material mind to accommodate soul mind. With soul mind you view opposites within the larger framework of wholeness. For instance, you are an embodied soul. This is not a contradiction—it is a truth verifiable through an awareness of your self as the knower and the immaterial experiencer who happens to be in a material form. Seeing from a broader field of awareness enables you to think out of the box while in the box, so to speak.

I have found particularly useful a mind stretch exercise that came intuitively to me one day. While in the middle of a heated argument that triggered an unseemly emotional response, I suddenly unhooked from the drama and snapped out of my unconsciousness. I was able to observe the flurry of emotions occurring within my mind from a station of stable awareness outside of it.

At that very moment I knew that my lower mind was contained within a higher, aware, and loving mind. I no longer had to defend myself or prove I was right and the other person was wrong, because I knew that in my core I wasn't alone within myself.

In stretching your mind, you give your defended self a safe place in which to land and find solace. Fire receives water. You can end most disputes before they get out of hand and cause needless hurt. I have broken this method down into four easy steps. Whenever your emotions rise in the middle of a disagreement, do this:

1: Breathe slowly and naturally into your belly. Bring your attention from your self to your soul by mentally identifying with your silent witness rather than with your annoyed ego.

2: Tell yourself that your problem is not about the other person.

3: Take responsibility for any negative thoughts and feelings that happen to be arising within you.

4: Tell yourself that is doesn't matter what anyone else thinks, says, or does. All that matters right now is the knowledge that when you are in the clutches of your own material mind you are held captive. When you are led by your soul mind, on the other hand, you are free to respond in a hundred different ways.

Of course, this mind stretch practice in the midst of a drama doesn't always work immediately. In a highly stressful encounter when the intensity of your anger spikes and adrenaline is flooding your nervous system, become aware as quickly as possible of shallow and rapid breathing from your chest or throat.

Attaching your awareness to your breath, bring your breath downward to your gut as you slowly inhale and exhale. Relax your stomach muscles. If you have a mantra, use it. If you do not, use the number system, exhaling the number one in silence then exhaling the number two, then repeat as needed until you are grounded and can return to the situation with clarity and calm.

Mind yoga is not only meant for austere monks and recluses engaged in discerning the real from the false, illusion from reality. It is suited for anyone who wishes to expand their mind and also for the person whose unruly thoughts and feelings often get the best of them.

In soul journey 13, we will incorporate three techniques: breath, visualization, and an affirmation mantra. Experience the paradox that your material mind is within your soul mind, and your soul mind is within your material mind. Rooting your material mind in the expansive ground of your soul mind will give you more mental and emotional freedom.

SOUL JOURNEY 13
Stretching the Mind

MEDITATION

After you have found a place of external quiet, enter that internal place of silence, your breathing room. After placing your tongue gently on the roof of your mouth, inhale and exhale through your nostrils. This is your body's oxygen ventilation system. You will notice that by doing this in a relaxed manner your belly naturally expands on the inhalation and contracts on the exhalation, ridding your body of carbon dioxide. Sense the cold air as you breathe in, and sense the warm air as you breathe out. Your mind is right where it needs to be now: focused and present. Do this for ten cycles or more.

Awakening Exercise

As you slowly inhale, picture a spaciousness that stretches out in a clockwise motion from your head to an expanse outside of your body as far as you can imagine. As you exhale, picture the circle getting smaller in size until it diminishes to a point at the center of your brain.

When you are ready, make this mental shift: on the inhale, picture that point inside your brain becoming an expanding circle, filling your entire body. On the exhale, imagine that spaciousness extending through the pores of your skin outward into space. Do this for five cycles or more.

Next, take the following affirmation mantra and use it in this way: On the inhale, silently say to yourself, "I am within infinite consciousness." On the exhale, silently say to yourself, "and infinite consciousness is within me." Do this for five cycles or more.

If you wish, you can bring the last portion of this exercise into your day today. Set for yourself a reminder at three separate intervals. At each signal, silently repeat the above mantra once or more.

CHAPTER 14
Heart Yoga

THE WAKEFUL SOUL KNOWS that they are always in the crucible of love in some form, even if it is a longing for a love lost or one not yet experienced. This universal condition only becomes heart yoga when it is chosen as an intentional path to become a more loving being.

The lower the vibration of love, the more a heart is likely to be mired in compromise, obligation, and negotiation. The higher the vibration, the less the dynamic of love is governed by habits and patterns bound by the desire to gain control or the desire to gain approval.

On the path of the heart, you have entered a long mountainous road with many twists and turns. In any intimate partnership there will be periods of loneliness and other times when you will feel a deep and abiding connection with the other.

Expect periods of unfulfilled longing and also heavenly times of bliss. Hurts can be transformed into forgiveness, one of the highest of soul senses cultivated on the heart path. Forgiveness frees the soul from the clutches of a constricted heart.

Any feeling—whether of low or high vibration—can be used to stretch the heart well beyond its narrow boundaries. To start on this path you only have to be right where you are. Heart yoga is the practice of growing the heart until it is capable of becoming one with the essence of love itself. Love tends to seek a vessel large enough to contain it. A small heart can sabotage love from achieving its full expression because it lacks the courage required of it to outgrow itself.

What we call love is most often just another form of dependency. Soul-to-soul love stretches the hearts of individuals in its embrace. Falling in love with another is easy. To become a life companion with love itself is difficult. To lose the self in another before one discovers their individual soul can weaken the physical heart. To find the self through a soulful life shared with another will strengthen the heart, however long that life with another lasts.

On the heart path, one quickly learns that obligatory love feels inauthentic. Love and obligation are contradictory terms. Soulful love cannot be forced, only freely given and received. And there is no force more quickly capable of freeing the heart than the flame of soulful love.

You can never be a victim of love if you allow love to do its work. Love's great labor is to slay your small heart to win the big heart of your soul.

Sometimes love will change its form in the middle of a life shared by two. One may outgrow the other when they are starving for soulful connection. Another may find it difficult to accept that love often changes form. Where love is concerned, there are no guarantees. Love will take a soul where love wishes if the soul gives its assent.

Only your soul can discern whether your heart is being diminished or augmented in a relationship. Ask whether a relationship is growing your heart or draining it of its life force. Small love is safe. Succumbing to the need for security also weakens the heart. Big love is risky and will happily break open your small heart to accommodate your soul. Should you choose heart yoga, do so because of your desire to widen your heart's borders, with a companion or not.

You may be experiencing loneliness without a partner due to loss by illness, death, or divorce. Never believe for a second that love has forsaken you. Love as love will never abandon you. Love may just want a deeper intimacy with you so needs to wound you so that you can become more loving. There is great wisdom in opening to love and letting go with love. When practiced as a yoga, love will flow back to you a hundredfold.

In soul journey 14, you are led through a heart stretch exercise. An effective way to relieve yourself and the world of mental suffering is to focus your attention on the receiving and giving of love. This practice expands and strengthens the heart of your soul.

SOUL JOURNEY 14
Stretching the Heart

MEDITATION

After you find a fitting place of quiet, sit comfortably. Close your eyes and enter that safe inner space, your breathing room within. After you take several relaxed breaths into your belly, bring your awareness to your heart. When you inhale, imagine that you are breathing into your physical heart. When you exhale, visualize that you are breathing into the deep space at your heart's center just beyond its borders. Do this for several cycles.

AWAKENING EXERCISE

Continue the practice of breathing into your heart. As you inhale, picture the quiet strength of your breath expanding the spiritual heart within your physical heart. As you exhale, see and feel your heart being filled with love.

As you inhale and exhale, visualize this love as so abundant that it pours out of the borders of your body and into the immediate environment outside of you. See and feel this love extending outward, embracing all of your loved ones.

Keep expanding your heart for as long as you wish, seeing and feeling your big heart pouring out its love to everyone in the universe, to strangers, to those whom you may not like or who have injured you. Imagine your big heart filling the earth and the skies and universe with each exhalation.

Now picture yourself relaxing and coming home to that spiritual heart of your soul that dwells deep within the physical heart of your body. Feel the cleansing, warm light of this love inundate your entire being.

Open your eyes now and rest in the flow of this love. Emanate kindness to everything and to everyone you encounter today. Whenever you feel low, go to the well of that heart within your heart and take in its energy. Share cups of it freely. You have found an endless well.

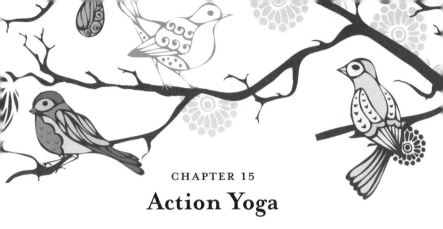

CHAPTER 15

Action Yoga

ACTIONS THAT CREATE DRAMAS imprison the soul in the worst of what the material world has to offer. Dramas pull you out of presence where the soul lives. In moments of practicing presence, you are roasting the seeds of thoughts before they can flourish into actions that produce automatic responses.

Automatic responses are habits of unconscious desiring, mentally accepted programs of thought and behavior. Programs of behavior produce artificial humans. An artificial human is not a modern creation but has existed since the birth of the false self. The false self is the shadow of the soul. When the false self acts, it does so in the shadow of presence.

The false self moves like the pendulum of a clock, attaching to objects of pleasure and avoiding objects of pain. In contrast, intervening on this imprisoning pattern sets the mind free. You are no longer driven by likes and dislikes. Presence is the one place where the dramas of attachment and aversion are refused entry.

If you wish to practice action yoga, here are some simple soulful doings you can install:

- Wash your own dishes with the presence of soul mind. Make your bed with conscious care. Fold your clothes and let the smell of cleanliness and the aura of orderliness establish a tone for your day.
- Schedule a regular activity for the sheer joy of it rather than for the money or recognition it will bring.
- Do the next right thing for yourself and don't worry about what others are doing or not doing.
- Experience the soulful actions of patience and waiting.
- Sit quietly for a few minutes, resting in simple awareness.
- Take a walk in presence. Whether you are on a city street, a country road, a beach, or a forest path, walk naturally, at a slower pace. Don't let the churning thoughts of your mind rush your body along. Bring your focused awareness to one of your five senses. Set your cell phone to ring in five minutes while you bring your attention to the sense of sight, then five minutes for smell, five for hearing, five for taste, and then five for touch. If you choose to focus on just one

physical sense, pick one that you feel will bring you most quickly into presence.

- Reach out to someone in physical, mental, emotional, or spiritual need without thought of benefit or return. Practice moments of unconditional kindness. These moments can thread themselves into a seamless life of unconditional love.
- Wherever you happen to be, with soulful intention, hold the presence of positivity for five minutes.

Action yoga is similar to the natural light in nature that saturates all creation with its rays whether it is day or night. Return to the now that is always here and to the here that is always now. Return to your center when you become aware that you are off base. Return to mindfulness when you become aware that you are on automatic. Return, and return again and again to presence. As long as we have a material mind, we will always need to return to soul mind. Soul mind is where presence lives, moves, and has its being.

Soulful doing has a tendency to not create new bindings. Bindings are the result of thoughts, words, and deeds that hold the mind in a state of entrapment, stealing freedom and serenity away from us. Whenever we perform the simplest of actions in presence, we have an abiding sense of peace and an enduring feeling of happiness.

In soul journey 15, we are guided to a mindfulness state where we can easily identify more and more with our essence. Resting in presence in the midst of activity, we connect with our soul mind that always lives in a state of relaxed alertness, no matter what is happening. This is effective mental hygiene.

SOUL JOURNEY 15
Soulful Presence

MEDITATION

As soon as you find a quiet place to sit, with your eyes open, take two or three strong breaths, enough to feel your chest expand. This will give you a sense of immediate presence because your breath, your body, and awareness are now in conscious connection.

Close your eyes and enter your breathing room. As you breathe naturally, inhaling on the rise of your breath and exhaling on the fall of your breath, listen gently to all external sounds that emerge. When you find yourself pulled into the drama of thought forms (future or past) allow this listening to the external sounds to bring you back into the moment.

Do this for five or more minutes. Continue with the exercise on the next page.

Awakening Exercise

Do this entire exercise with your eyes open. Look around the room where you happen to be. Sense that presence that lives behind the superficial present within and around you. Picture your worrying self fade into the background and just be with everything in an accepting way.

Now look out the nearest window. Open it if this is possible. Whatever sights and sounds are in the vicinity, take them in with the presence of positivity and the positivity of presence.

Stay in this long moment of presence. Whether you are washing your hands, eating, opening and closing doors, do every little thing with mindfulness today. No matter how many others you meet today, have no expectation from them. See them from a place of presence.

When you go outside to begin your day in the world, use every moment as a practice of presence.

Your entire life is the real moment. Cultivate this soulful doing by becoming a companion of being. Be with others and with the world today in presence. Your one accomplishment is to return as many times as you need to the practice of presence.

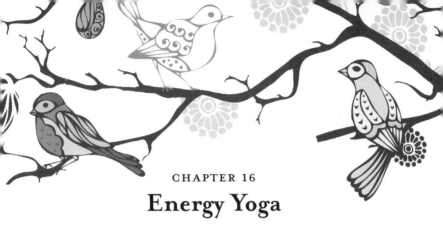

CHAPTER 16
Energy Yoga

ENERGY YOGA REASONABLY BEGINS with a positive approach to the body and to ordinary life. Above all, the path of energy is the practice of beginning and ending each day with a clear-minded and clear-hearted attitude toward life.

Yet, a positive approach to life doesn't magically happen. You have to bring positivity to the moment. You must take responsibility for the quality of energy that you are bringing into yourself and putting out into the world.

Deepen your understanding of the relationship between energy and awareness. When energy is instilled with awareness, and awareness is enlivened with energy, the body and mind are clarified and cleansed, like a spring-fed lake.

The goal of energy yoga is for the body to be entirely permeated with the consciousness of the soul. In the West, we associate such practices with kundalini yoga. *Kundalini* is Sanskrit for "coiled one." Coiled at the base of the spine, the energy of light waits to be activated through breath-awareness techniques. Much has been written about the psychological instability that can occur when the nervous system is not prepared for the sudden release of kundalini energy through intensely focused breath control practices over a short period of time.

For safety purposes, I recommend a gradual approach, such as the soft martial arts of tai chi, aikido, or qigong (also known as ch'i kung). Although I have familiarity with tai chi and aikido, I have been practicing qigong (most often translated "energy work") for many years. The energy work of qigong has an external component (waigong) and more importantly, an internal component (neigong).

Similar to tai chi—and considered by some to be a more ancient form of it—qigong begins with waigong, the circulation of the breath in coordination with body postures and movements. After increased skill the practitioner may proceed to neigong: the refinement of vital essence (jing), into subtle energy essence (qi), and ultimately into spiritual essence (shen).

The cultivation of focus (attention), will (intention), and recollection (retention)—A-I-R—is instrumental in energy yoga. Whichever energy yoga you choose, it is imperative that you bring these three principles into your meditation and accompanying visualization practices.

To focus your energy, direct it by cultivating the power of concentration. To will your energy, bring a sense of purposefulness to your practice. To recollect your energy, gather it through conscious movement that brings the mind and body together, working harmoniously as an ensemble, as a team in alliance.

Remember that energy is always available to us, waiting to receive either the higher intelligence of the soul mind or the lower intelligence of the material mind. Intelligence is light manifesting as power. This is one of the underlying secrets of kundalini. Kundalini is divine-light-energy waiting to manifest

Energy yoga slowly dissolves the boundaries of the limited mind, assimilating it to the unlimited mind of the soul. Only the soul mind can balance, channel, and harmonize the split energy that the material mind produces. Split energy creates the opposites of winning and losing, domination and subjugation, control and submission.

The Tao is the eternal movement of apparent opposites mirrored perfectly in nature as the undivided and harmonious motion of eternal becoming. Energy yoga works to unite with the great flow, with the energy of oneness, the Tao.

As the material mind gradually identifies with the great flow, it dissolves into the mind of the soul and ultimately into the soul of souls, infinite consciousness. Infinite consciousness manifests in each individual soul and in all creation as divine-light-energy.

In soul journey 16, we envision the primary goal of energy yoga: to help awaken us to the reality that the material world, including the earth itself, is permeated with flowing kundalini, with divine-light-energy.

Unite with the Flow

MEDITATION

Enter your breathing room within. Align your awareness to the natural rhythm of the rise and fall of your breath, for your breath is that one, continuous event that occurs twenty-four hours a day in your body.

Whenever your awareness drifts away from its soft focus upon the subtleties of your body's natural breathing rhythm, say to yourself, "thinking," and then return to the practice of simple presence, of your awareness following each unique breath. Feel your soul nature, the basic goodness of your being, and your kinship with the harmonious in-breath and out-breath of the natural universe.

Continue this breathing practice for five minutes or more.

AWAKENING EXERCISE

Now, picture every molecule of your breath being washed in the light of higher consciousness. See this light as the energy of your soul that is connected to the source of light itself.

Stay with this image: that your breath right now that is flowing through your body—from head to toe—is being infused with the breath of spirit, with the energy and light of the source of consciousness.

Let this light move through the central column of your spine, breathing upward from your feet to the top of your head and breathing downward from the top of your head to your feet.

Feel the healing balm of this ointment of ointments, as your entire body is washed in this divine-light-energy.

CHAPTER 17
Beauty Yoga

THE PATH OF BEAUTY depicts the soul's profound appreciation for its embodied life in the material world. Whenever someone encounters something they regard as beautiful, the accompanying feeling is the momentary bliss of exhilaration.

The soul's existence in a physical body glimpses, touches, smells, tastes, and attunes to that perfection in the curve of a seashell, in the texture of a stem, in the aroma of an herb, in the sweetness of fruit, and in the sound of a well-struck chord. Long before the child utters its first word, its soul knows the language of beauty in nature's flutter of a breeze, in the pitter-patter of rainfall, in the lilt of birdsong, and in the whir of a bee's wing.

We experience beauty as we pass through this world, whether slowly or swiftly. This is perhaps why we behold a treasured piece of gold or silver, a diamond or ruby, a river stone or a shard of colored glass with unspeakable splendor.

All living things under the heavens constantly radiate the beauty of their essence under the ancient sun that descends and rises anew each day. It is our joyful task to keep every one of our senses wide open to every moment that lies in wait to reveal and bestow its wealth to us. We accomplish this by activating the great sense of the soul. The great sense of the soul savors human existence and absorbs every bit of life into its pores like a sponge.

The savoring sense also has the capacity to perceive the energy within things and whether certain energies are medicinal or toxic. A seeker who is practiced in beauty yoga associates ugliness with the inner architecture of bad energy. Bad energy is bent and misshapen. Bad energy lacks flow, smooth lines, and is absent of grace and poise. Bad energy attacks when disturbed, lashes out, punctures, and drains.

When we become soul-sensitive, what appears to us as repulsive has little to do with outer forms unless these forms are manifesting a negative interior. Much of what we perceive as outwardly ugly may be no more than the preferences of the collective material mind each of us are programmed into.

The sun reveals itself in a spectrum of colors before it rises and sets. Its golden radiance appears and disappears and permeates its rays through endless blooming clouds. When the moon has waned, the night veils our eyes from the earth. When it is full, a shawl of light falls ever so lightly across the surface of rock, flower, tree, sky, and ocean.

The path of beauty evokes wonderment because the soul is overcome by beauty's magnificence. In every concealing another revealing of beauty's visage dawns. Beauty ravishes and delights the soul. Perhaps this is why beauty and bliss resemble one another. Bliss is the soul's intimate dalliance with body and ultimately with all of what is juicy and earthy.

A seeker attracted to the path of beauty opens wide all of the soul's senses, and all of the body's senses, to fully experience every moment with soulful pleasure.

In soul journey 17, you will practice the opening of all of your soul's senses to experience the delight of being in your body and on this earth.

SOUL JOURNEY 17
The Great Sense

MEDITATION

Find a fitting place that is calling you inward. Enter your breathing room today with eyes open.

As you breathe in through your nostrils and into your belly, exhale down all the way to your toes.

Consciously open all of your senses of sight, hearing, taste, touch, and smell as you complete several in-breath/out-breath cycles.

Awakening Exercise

Activate the great sense within you, that symphony of your soul's senses of sight, hearing, taste, touch, and smell.

Open your mind to the beautiful, whatever the highest version of that word means to you.

Attune to whatever song or melody that is agreeable to you and gives you a sense of harmony.

Resonate with that vibration and feel the bliss of the deep hum within you at the core of your being.

Savor beauty's sweetness in a form you can conjure, like milk or honey.

Take in also the aroma of beauty as you would the perfume of your favorite flower.

Bring all of these senses to the center of your heart where your soul lives, breathes, and enjoys its being.

Call forth every one of your soul's senses to conjoin into the unity of the great sense.

Fill your body from head to toe with the life of your soul that itself is a perfect reflection of beauty-in-the-making.

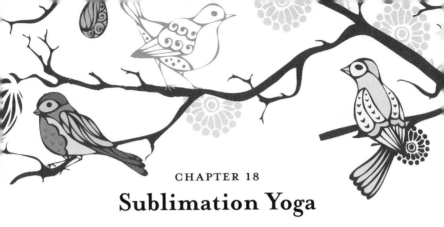

CHAPTER 18

Sublimation Yoga

SUBLIMATION YOGA ASKS THAT we wait and watch until the right opportunity presents itself. A soul on this path desires to cultivate a sublime (or purified) mind. We often mistake the idea of purifying our thoughts as an exercise in shaming ourselves for what we "shouldn't" think. Purification needs to be taken out of its morality box and understood in the context of sublimation. To purify means to detox, to cleanse, and to clarify awareness with patience and warrior-like vigilance. Again and again, nature is the best teacher in matters of the soul.

The twelve steps of Alcoholics Anonymous is a modern example of the sublimation path. In twelve-step meetings, you are encouraged to "work the steps" by naming your inner stuff, accepting your inner stuff, cleaning your inner stuff, and letting go of the inner stuff you don't need anymore. It has become a simple and effective spiritual path for many in the modern world, regardless of whether there happens to be an addiction issue. I have often suggested the twelve steps for those who prefer a non-religious path with psychological depth.

Sublimation yoga is particularly useful for those who are struggling with addictions to drugs, alcohol, food, sex, and gambling. One of the surest ways of weakening a negative habit is by redirecting one's energy resourcefully. A negative mood can be a catalyst for a creative response if I learn to trust that taking positive action reinforces inner changes in myself. Positive external actions tend to create positive internal states.

Fasting is also a technique that can be incorporated in sublimation yoga but with common sense and (if warranted), conducted under the supervision of a trained health practitioner or therapist. Fasting from social media, cell phones, computers, and television for periods of time detoxifies the mind.

One of most effective fasting practices is the internal kind: abstaining from negative thoughts, withdrawing from inner dramas, and detaching from our own private inner movies. There is nothing that connects us more immediately to the heart and to being than mental fasting. It is best to detach from all activity produced by the material mind that disturbs and causes inner strife. Life will bring enough challenges to us; fretting and worrying are useless and drain the soul of precious energy.

In spiritual psychology, sublimating the energy of thoughts is a healthy alternative to repressing energy. For example, when sex energy or any emotionally charged impulse is channeled into higher awareness rather than repressed, a sense of well-being arises.

When I was a monk, some of the ways that I learned to sublimate and elevate sex energy were through meditation practices, monastic studies, walking in the forest, running, working in the fields, singing, playing a musical instrument, keeping a journal, and writing poetry. It took years before I learned that sex is primal spirit and spirit is refined sex. Sex and spirit are two different forms of the same elixir.

Any method that seeks the cleansing and refinement of consciousness is the yoga of the sublimation path. Poets have used the term "crucible" to describe the tests and trials in human life that shape a human being for the better. A crucible is a vessel made to withstand high temperatures when a substance is heated within it. There is an alchemical process that happens within the crucible that blends the substances inside. After being heated at extreme temperatures, something wholly new and stronger emerges.

Accepting all conditions posed by the circumstances of daily life is an opportunity to practice sublimation yoga.

Every life challenge is energy waiting to be understood, unblocked, and uplifted.

In soul journey 18, we are led through a practice based on the earth principle, "Energy changes form." Cleansing the material mind through the detoxing power of the soul mind raises our energy, clarifies our thoughts, and refines our emotions.

SOUL JOURNEY 18
Energy Cleanse

MEDITATION

Find a place where you can sit quietly. Close your eyes and enter your breathing room. Bring the inner gaze of your attention to your body and perform a scan, locating any place of tension manifesting in your muscles or joints.

Scan now your mood. Accept however you feel on the spectrum of high or low, clean or toxic energy. Relax your eyes, mouth and jaw, chest, and stomach as you breathe deeply inhaling and exhaling through your nose. Bring kind awareness into your entire body and wash yourself with this cleansing light for ten breath cycles.

AWAKENING EXERCISE

As you breathe naturally and without force, imagine that every molecule of your body is being cleansed with the breath of your soul. Do this until you feel even a slight shift in your inner energy field.

Continue your deep breathing. Think of a difficult situation or a problem you are having in your life.

Notice how you might be doing the same thing and expecting different results.

Play with ideas of how you might do just one thing differently or how you might approach this situation with an attitude of openness.

As you go about your day today, practice flexibility in your movements and also in your conversation with others. Listen. Stay open to receive the solution to your problem. This receptivity of soul will allow a shift of energy to emerge naturally.

CHAPTER 19

Integrative Yoga

A SEEKER'S DESIRE AND decision to practice two or more yogas sets them solidly on the path of integration. This will happen naturally, gradually, and according to the soul's nature, interest, psychological needs, and spiritual stage of growth. The seasoned soul will often take up an integrative yoga in order to develop and coordinate the mind, the heart, and the body.

A beginner who is primarily mind-directed or heart-directed may wisely choose to focus exclusively on a specific yoga. However, at some point in your path you may have a strong desire to balance and strengthen both the heart and the mind. If so, the integrative path of combining the mind and the heart yogas will benefit you.

Sometimes adding one or more yogas to an already established practice is necessary for your optimum mental and emotional wellness. You may be drawn to the action yoga of serving others in need or practicing selfless doing for its own sake, for example. The mind and energy yogas would replenish your energy and help you to establish clearer boundaries in both your personal and professional life. Taking extended periods of time for deeper introspection or to experience a deeper connection with the flow of nature enriches a life devoted to selfless action.

If you find that you are in a period of your life where you are receiving challenge after challenge, with little time to take a breath, it may be your karma to embrace the sublimation path. If you undertake this yogic way it will be beneficial to incorporate lessons from the warrior's energy path. A secondary yoga of energy—for example, a qigong regimen—helps to offset the potential dangers of negative stress caused by the curveballs and minefields that come your way.

When in the midst of life's intense struggles that can wear you down, adding heart yoga helps to raise your spirits through the cultivation of empathy and love. Beauty yoga teaches how to savor and appreciate life's wonders always there at your fingertips and around every corner. These yogas are healthy supplements to the mind, action, and energy paths.

Speaking with a trusted guide or a seasoned soul about the integrative path can help you discern which yogas have the most charm and are most useful both for your soul's hygiene and for your stage of growth. You can also ask for inner guidance while in meditation as to which additional yoga might serve to increase your soul's consciousness, connect you to the earth and the world, and to others around you in the healthiest ways.

When you have become soul conscious, a path will eventually get your attention and speak to you. Its particular scent will draw you to investigate the paths you are drawn to exploring. Your soul will always be led to what it needs for its own growth. Reading about the journeys of other great souls, their descents and ascents, ups and downs, twists and turns on the royal road of the yogas may encourage and inspire you to a particular integrative path.

Whatever combination of yogas you may choose to practice, all that really matters is how much they assist you in enlarging your being so that you are able to accommodate more light and positive energy, thereby making more soul sense of your life.

In soul journey 19, you are led on a journey of thanks for the gift of your soul, the soul's senses, and the variety of pathways that are available to you. As you gain more familiarity with the pathways, you will come to know which ones speak to you and call forth the best in you.

SOUL JOURNEY 19
Making Soul Sense of the Yogas

MEDITATION

Go to a space that has an aura of quietude about it and emits good energy. Sit comfortably. Close your eyes, and enter the welcoming atmosphere of your breathing room.

Bring your awareness to the breathing in and breathing out of positive energy as light throughout your body.

When thoughts come, gently turn your attention back to your breath. Feel the relaxing and healing effect of this conscious breathing of positive energy as it infuses your body and your mind. Do this for five minutes or more.

AWAKENING EXERCISE

As you focus on the inhalation and exhalation of energy throughout your body, imagine this energy as light within you. This living light invigorates and illuminates your path as you continue your meditation, study, and application of the yogas in a way that makes soul sense to you.

Give thanks to the source of your curiosity that has led you to discover more about the yogas. Know that this source has been with you from the beginning of your journey and will accompany you throughout. You have activated the multiple senses of your soul and more. You have also fortified and expanded some of your soul's senses through the giving and receiving of insight, empathy, and presence. You are making more soul sense of your life.

Although you have many more soul awakenings to experience, for today, rest in this gratitude for how far you have come on your journey. Enjoy experimenting with the principles of these yogas and applying them to your daily life.

Bring this affirmation with you today: "I am awakening more and more to the soul that I am becoming."

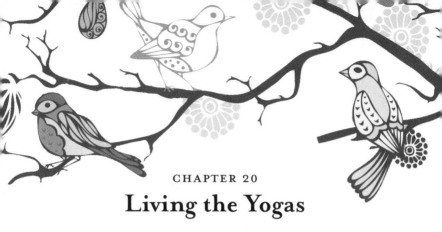

CHAPTER 20

Living the Yogas

FROM THE MOMENT A seeker makes some headway in the practice of any of the yogas, life begins to change from the inside out and from the outside in. Once you have certain knowledge that your soul is your strength, you will feel the flow of your soul's life force. This is your spirit. The spirit of your soul is the all-pervasive current of energized peace, a calming stream of refreshing serenity.

It is impossible to overestimate the results of serenity. Serenity is not static, but dynamic. Energized peace comes as soon as we root ourselves in the unifying force of soul through the yogas. The energized peace of serenity emerges when the powers within your body, mind, and heart are quickened with the spirit, the lifeblood of the soul.

When through the yogas you have become grounded in your soul, you will also feel the containment of your soul's skin, bones, and marrow. From such a place of inner strength, you will no longer need to defend and protect yourself from the onslaughts of the material world. The yogas give you entry to nature's maturing field of force that weaves the very fabric of your soul's unique substance.

That is why in addition to giving you serenity, the yogas gradually strip away all that is false about you. Your false self believes that integrity is something to be attained. However, your true self knows that the integrity of you is actually the starting point, not some end result.

We don't question the truth of the flower, the tree, the river, the sky, or an animal that walks across the earth or swims in the ocean. This is because nature is completely immersed in the spirit and light of soul.

The yogas remove obstructions to the light of your soul that wants to shine into your body, mind, and heart. It is through this light that you receive messages—intuitions— from your soul about how best to improve the quality of your inner and outer life.

The yogas develop intuition to the highest possible level. This is because your soul's senses of sight, hearing, taste, smell, and touch are the channels to intuitive knowledge. Through intuition you receive information about the integrative nature of the soul and how the yogas serve to connect the soul to the physical body and the material world.

Seeds of wisdom are being planted within you. The yogas generate these seeds. As you grow your soul's intelligence, you become more able to discern all things and make your way through the world with the simplicity of presence. Presence rids you of unnecessary baggage. What remains is your true being: the substance, blood, bone, and marrow of your soul.

Knowing who you are, you no longer need to place your trust in someone else. By placing your trust in your own soul you come to realize that others will speak, think, feel and behave according to their level of knowledge and wisdom. Your only concern is to root yourself in the fertile soil of the yogas, where the soul's senses may flourish.

In soul journey 20 you are led through a soul scan. It is important to ask questions about your own life from that inner place of intuitive and trusting soulfulness. In this way, seeds of wisdom will blossom into their fullness and you will become a blessing for the world.

SOUL JOURNEY 20
Soul Scan

MEDITATION

Locate a fitting place where you can sit undisturbed. Close your eyes and enter your breathing room within.

Follow your breath with your awareness. Relax your stomach muscles as you inhale deep into your belly. As you exhale, feel your stomach gently compress.

As thoughts enter your mind, let them come and go as they please. All you have to do is bring your awareness back to your breath if you find yourself attaching to any of them.

Feel the cleansing flow of oxygen throughout your body. Within this oxygen is spirit, the breath of your soul. Spirit provides your soul with the nutrients it needs to thrive. Connect consciously with the breath of your soul for five minutes.

Awakening Exercise

Take a moment to ask these questions: Am I listening to my soul? Am I hearing my soul's words of encouragement and challenge? Am I on the right path? Is there something I need to adjust or change about my approach to life with the help of yogas?

Do I feel the energized peace of my soul's spirit flowing within me? Do I radiate and project this serenity to others? Am I welcoming to all whom I encounter because I trust in my own soul? Do I behold others with unconditional appreciation, intuitively knowing they are where they need to be? How do I hold myself accountable to my soul?

Do I approach the world with the spirit of simplicity? Am I making more soul sense of the world?

Rest in the inner silence of listening to your soul's answers. You may feel a prompting to journal an insight that may come.

Let your soul nature guide you with its light. Trust the senses and spirit of your soul. They are being fortified to direct your soul in every encounter with the material world. Seeds of wisdom are being planted in your soul at this moment. You will be learning more about how to ripen these seeds to their utmost potential.

PART THREE
Bringing Soul to the Material World

EVERY SEEKER YEARNS FOR soulful companionship. Relationships shape the soul's path and its destiny. You will find your soul's purpose within every single encounter in the material world. Your soul has created every one of your fellow seekers and they have created you. Every soul, including every creature and the earth itself, is a soul mentor, instructing you in the manifold ways of love and knowledge.

Look around you. You see that you are among countless souls of varying degrees of soul consciousness. Once you have identified your own place as a seeking soul in the world, you will become more able to assist others to find their place in it as well.

To become soul conscious means that the choice is always yours to make use of each and every occurrence to your soul's advantage. As you become more soul realized, you welcome and learn to skillfully handle the stresses that come with being an embodied soul in the material world.

Since we know that unfoldment is impossible unless we are willing to be embodied, we must strive to always be here now, as a soul in a physical body among other souls in a physical body. Once we have established the centrifugal force of soulfulness we will less likely be pulled from soul mind into material mind.

A tree must root itself in the earth before its branches can reach to the sky. The soul needs grounding to flourish, and our relationships serve to accomplish this and much more. Relationships that call forth the soul teach us how to love others not for what we see in them but for who they really are.

Once the soul has planted its essence into the fertile earth, it will find soul-enriching relationships that inspire and help it to unfurl its unique sun-filled blossoms toward the awaiting heavens.

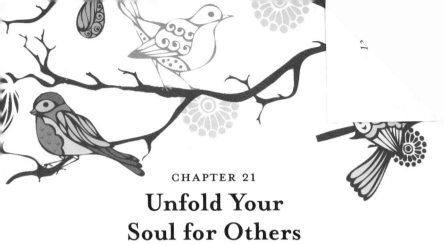

CHAPTER 21

Unfold Your Soul for Others

YOU WILL HAVE SOMETHING worthy to give when you have become something worthy to your own being. True worthiness cannot come from the fabricated self. Worthiness arises naturally from deep within your core. It is as fresh as a spring-fed lake and as sweet as the sap tapped from the maple tree and boiled in the sugarhouse.

Genuine self-esteem quenches the thirst of everyone it encounters and sweetens the palette of everything it touches. From the soul-centered place of genuineness you can observe without judgment everything that is happening: that all events are presented to us in order to serve the purpose of either our fabricated self or our soul.

An individual in the making has no investment in changing anyone else or their agenda. Don't try to change others. Just become yourself. In so doing, you will join the living. And having joined the living, you can now become more of yourself. You can now be of real use to the world.

The fabricated self is similar to an inflated balloon. There are so many different balloons of many colors that we send up in the sky so everyone can see. "Oh, look at my balloon!" "Mine can go higher than yours." "I am so sad, my balloon is so small and puny." "Hey, you just punctured my balloon!" and so on.

The soul, on the other hand, is like a tree rising slowly and surely in the forest. If a storm—or a human—uproots the tree, it will become a home for creatures or persons, perhaps a bed, a table, a chair, or even a musical instrument. A tree always finds its way somehow to new life because it is real.

For humans, on the other hand, realness has to be excavated. To forge your identity is perhaps one of the greatest selfless acts you will ever achieve. Becoming your soul takes immense internal strength.

It is not only your body that has its own unique thumbprint—your soul does too. In fact, the singularity that characterizes the body is a hint that the soul, as well, cannot be reduplicated.

However, your fabricated self is the epitome of reduplication and programming. It is the only quantifiable and anonymous thing about you, even though it wants to think that it is unique.

Deep down, the fabricated self knows it can't get the job of embodiment and unfoldment accomplished. It needs help. Unless it reaches inward for higher assistance, the self will become the great imposter.

As soon as you get on the path of becoming genuine, others around you will follow, others who also want to become genuine. What do you have to offer the world? Something impenetrable. Once you get on the path of embodiment and unfoldment, others around you will pick up on the vibration.

Embodiment is presence. When you are in presence you feel totally alive. Unfoldment is freedom. To feel the soul increasing in vigor and strength is liberating. By mirroring to others what a path of presence and freedom looks like, others will want to find their path of trueness too.

No one needs another absent, programmed self. No one needs another negative, imprisoned self. No one needs another oppositional, whining self. No one needs another balloon full of unconscious air. What the world needs is an awakened you, a human being fully alive, breathing with oxygen made intelligent, breathing with chi, with prana, with spirit.

Become this being and you will look within everything that you see with the laser sight of your soul. You will see that inside of them lives a tree with deep roots in the ground, and with a trunk and branches of every imaginable shape and size, gradually rising, rising high into the sky.

In soul journey 21, you will visualize your soul's deeper embodiment of presence in the body and the ongoing unfoldment of freedom into your individuality. This exercise will also help you to accept everything and everyone that appears in the world as significant for your soul's growth.

SOUL JOURNEY 21
Soul Tree

MEDITATION

Find a comfortable place to sit quietly. Close your eyes. Enter your breathing room. Take two strong breaths, inhaling through your nose and exhaling through your mouth. This will engage both your mind and your body in the most simple and immediate way.

After this, return to your nasal breathing. Before you begin, gently rest the tip of your tongue on the roof of your mouth. Follow with your mind the rise of your breath when you inhale up your back to the roof of your mouth, and the fall of your breath on the exhale down your front to just below your navel. Do this for ten cycles.

AWAKENING EXERCISE

As you continue this focused orbit breathing, picture yourself as a little baby, your body strong and full of awe and wonder, full of blessing for the world. Stay with this image for several breaths.

Now, imagine that your body has transformed into a beautiful healthy tree, full of leaves with strong branches. From the earth, you breathe in moisture, up through the central column of your trunk to the tip of your highest branches and leaves, breathing out into the sky. Next, you breathe in the pure light from the sky into your highest branches and leaves, breathing out and down the central column of your trunk, to its roots. Do this for five to ten breath cycles or more.

Slowly open your eyes…connect once again to your surroundings. Feel the renewal and refreshment from this exercise and bring the feeling of refreshing water and light into your day today.

Occasionally remind yourself to take just one minute of inner quiet, even if you're walking around or sitting down, busy with your thoughts.

Align your thoughts with the truth of your being and your becoming.

With your eyes opened or closed, breathe in and out this affirmation deep into your core:

I embody presence and unfold my soul in freedom for the betterment of all living things. I bring to myself everything and everyone for my soul's growth and therefore, I am happy.

CHAPTER 22

Share Your Light

IN THE FAMOUS Lord of the Rings trilogy, the fiction writer J.R.R. Tolkien ingeniously described the dangers of power. Not only in the realm of the imagination but also in the material world there is a universal battle going on between darkness and light, between power-hungry selves and path-hungry souls.

When you awaken to the wayfarer's journey, you feel a kinship with Bilbo Baggins in Tolkien's tale *The Hobbit*. Bilbo uncharacteristically sets out on an adventure. His bravery is put to the test. Similarly, once on the path of the wayfarer, you discover that you are on a hero's quest. That quest is for the treasure of inner light that only your wakeful soul can find. If hoarded, this light will dim. Light grows by letting it do what it does best. Light loves to illuminate and bestow life.

The more light a soul accesses, the more illuminating and bestowing it becomes. This is what awakening looks like. When you awaken to your gift, you will know what you are supposed to bring to the world. Your soul's inborn talent will also help you gain new powers. Bilbo acquired a magic ring that, when worn, would render him invisible to his opponents.

Your soul's gift is a power, a key of light. It is a charism. Charism derives from the Greek word "charis" (meaning grace, kindness, and life). For the ancient Greeks, a charism was considered a gift bestowed by a divine force that drew others toward them. The soul draws others toward them because it emanates such a charism.

Practicing the yogas assist you in finding your gift, your key of light. The yogas teach you how to use that gift, that power, for the sake of others. Helping a soul find their internal gift gives them a key of light that unlocks a door to their own powers. They are forever transformed when this happens. Help someone find their inborn gift and they will depend less upon you and more upon their own soul.

As a soulful being, you will become a lighter of souls. Your soul's light is as natural as the moon that shines. Radiate this light to the world around you. Radiance is the opposite of vanity. Vanity is the shadow of light and only dimly lights up the self.

Your soul will be known by the quantity and quality of light it diffuses. The material-driven ones are in dire need of the soul-driven ones. The soul-driven have learned to see the true inner light that emanates from inside a person.

There are other secrets yet to be revealed as you learn to see more by the light of your soul, secrets visible only to those that have found their key of light. This light is more powerful than the ignition key of warm consciousness that you received at the beginning of your journey. That key was for you. This key is for others.

In soul journey 22, you will be led on a visual journey to be given another important key. This key opens a door to your soul's gift, a power that you were meant to share with the world, an empowering light that enables you to illuminate and bestow what others most need.

SOUL JOURNEY 22
Key of Light

MEDITATION

Find a place of refuge free of external distractions. Sit quietly, and take two strong breaths. This will engage your mind with your body and usher you into immediate presence.

Close your eyes. Now you are here, in your internal place of refuge, your breathing room.

With your awareness, gently follow the natural rise and fall of your breath. Don't force anything. Without judgment, allow any thoughts and feelings that appear and disappear to strengthen and weaken as they will. Don't worry, for they are not real.

These thoughts and feelings are the inner winds that can cloud and darken the light of your soul. Acknowledge and accept them for what they are: only a passing show. Wait for the clouds to disperse and the light will shine naturally within your mind once again.

Awakening Exercise

Open your heart center now to receive another key of light from the source of your being. This key opens the door to a deeper place within your soul. This key is meant to light up either an unrecognized quality within yourself or one you might have taken for granted. Take this key in your hand. Receive it with openness and with gratitude. This is your key now.

Feel your key's power. It has been given to you to open the door into a deeper place within your soul for the sake of others. With your imagining ability now more seasoned, open this door with your key.

What do you see? Is there a talent that you have that you are cultivating? Are you hiding it? Are you avoiding it because of what this talent may ask of you? Simply rest with whatever comes up or does not.

Never mind if nothing yet arises in your consciousness. At the right time you will be connected with your unique charism. You will receive the help you need to find that treasure within you because the material world is in need of it. For now, simply open your eyes and look out into your world. Just be…and be enriched by the certainty that you have been given this key of light, that is a gift in and of itself.

CHAPTER 23

Mentoring the Soul

A SOUL MENTOR IS, first and foremost, a finder of light for souls who have misplaced theirs. The finder of light has acquired the skill of sensing with their soul. They can locate and rescue the dimmed light exiled in a cave inside of you.

Being a seasoned locator of inner light, the soul mentor first discovers then tends to your inner fire, breathing spirit into its embers. The soul mentor can also aid in the finding of inner water. Once a soul finds the nurturing well of life within themselves, a mentor can inspire them toward the highest goal they are capable of imagining. Those who have found the fire and water of their soul through the help of a mentor will seek to live according to the purpose of their soul's design.

A soul mentor helps you to claim the individuality of your soul, clarify your soul's intent, illuminate your soul's purpose, and stabilize your soul's passion. They can accomplish this because of their ability to soulfully hold space with you. This is a sacred space, a place where you may gradually create yourself in your own deepest image. The soul mentor creates with you a "breathing room" where your tired soul can go within to find untapped resources of energy. These resources provide the light of vision and also the water of refreshment.

The skill of creating and holding space for the soul can be imparted to any seasoned seeker. Soulful space is a force field of nonjudgmental acceptance, imparted to another through the soul's sense of touch. There is great healing in this simple but effective practice.

Holding soulful space with another gives them the freedom to allow the image of their soul to surface. Such freedom encourages a person to search and find solutions from within themselves. Soulful intimacy can occur when someone holds a contained atmosphere of quiet welcome. The encompassment of presence itself creates freedom and connection, acceptance and friendship. Genuine love is made in such a space.

In addition to the soul's sense of touch, the sense of soul sight has an important mentoring and healing role as well. Soul sight illuminates the darkness within. Darkness can provoke a sense of anxiety around the inner journey. Fear is a shadow of light, an ubiquitous entity that pervades until the light within you can enter and dissolve all clouds of doubt and uncertainty.

Your soul's light cleanses all toxic thoughts through its powerful presence in the mind. All of the soul journeys you have taken thus far at the end of each chapter underlie this core truth. There is nothing more effective in the healing process than the power of a correctly channeled will and rightful use of affirmation and visualization when put into accord with meditative breathing.

In addition to holding soulful presence with another, there are soul mentors who also happen to be gifted counselors. Any seasoned therapist will do as long as they are open to where you are on your path.

Since the soul mentor has acquired a measure of skill in helping to locate the true light within others and fostering that light, if you don't happen to have a soul mentor or therapist, do not be troubled. Trust that on this path of your soul's unfoldment you will always receive what and whom you need exactly at the right time when your soul is ready.

In soul journey 23, you are taught how to hold space for another. Often partners, friends, or family vent to one another, but without insight, without solution or purpose. The practice of holding soulful space with another is an effective tool for vanquishing darkness through the simple but powerful presence of emanating the soul's light.

SOUL JOURNEY 23
Holding Soulful Space for Another

MEDITATION

Go within, to your breathing room, that inner, soulful space that awaits you. Sit quietly with your eyes closed. Before you transition to relaxed breathing, take two strong breaths, enough to feel your chest expand to connect your body and your mind in simple presence with your surroundings.

Now, breathe naturally, bringing your awareness to the crown of your head on the inhale, following the exhale of your breath as it flows gently into your stomach.

AWAKENING EXERCISE

Imagine holding a space of acceptance in the presence of someone you know who needs this.

You sense their unquiet mind but rather than mirror their unrest, you become for them a quiet lake in which they can see their own reflection. They are calmed by the strength of your tranquility.

Imagine now holding a space of light in the presence of that person. You don't have to give them your own light.

You are just activating your light in that imaginal space you are holding for them.

Now, open your eyes and connect with your physical space. It is OK if this is only an idea for you right now. With practice you will be able to hold the space of unconditional acceptance for another. Sometimes it takes but a minute of soulful presence in someone's company before they start to feel a positive shift in their own energy.

As you go about your day, bring a spirit of spacious acceptance to each person you meet, as if you were the very green space for which everyone yearns.

CHAPTER 24

The Soul and Stress

THE SOUL GAINS STRENGTH through testing, much like the body's muscle is tested through applying conditions of stress. Without life's challenges, the inner fiber of the soul would weaken and atrophy. There are three inner qualities that the soul needs to cultivate to handle the stress of living in the material world: endurance, flexibility, and agility.

We gain endurance by containing and expending energy in measure. Endurance will get us through the long hauls in life. Marathons of any kind demand pacing, a balance of burning and cooling the energy that our body, mind, heart, and soul each express in different ways.

Before undertaking a physical challenge, we must listen to our body and slowly and steadily expand its power by burning (expending force) and cooling (relaxing force). When you burn, you build fire energy. When you cool, you restore water energy.

Meditation is also a burning and cooling practice. Concentrate your awareness on the movement of your breath without wavering your attention for a few minutes. This is the burning phase. Then, let your focus relax by allowing your thoughts to go where they want to. This is the cooling phase. Freedom to let your awareness roam after a concentrative period both clarifies and expands consciousness.

You can increase emotional endurance through a similar "burn and cool" exercise. Sit with your emotions at the soul level. Bring soulful presence to anger, to fear, to sorrow. This will eventually derail negative thoughts. As long as you don't fuel your emotions by thinking about them, you need not be concerned that your emotions will get the better of you. Just sit with them and observe them with neutral awareness. Soulful presence cools the heat of intense emotions.

Flexibility is another quality of soul that relieves stress. We generally associate flexibility with the looseness of our muscles and joints. In chapter 18, it was mentioned that any form of body yoga accomplishes a measure of physical and mental pliability. Using whatever means, practice being in your body with an attentive breathing mind, and this stream of intelligence will help to clear physical, mental, and emotional obstructions.

In its most refined form, flexibility is the capacity to adapt on the spot to any circumstance that arises. Once our entire being becomes more limber, we are better able to adapt to any situation with inner calm. The lesson here is simple: Think less. Be more. Thinking is burning. Being contains within itself both the flow of burning and the flow of cooling. This principle is exemplified in the fire, water, earth, and air elements as well as in the heating phase of day and the cooling phase of night.

A third way to alleviate the stress of navigating the material world is by developing agility. We most often associate agility with the body's swiftness, most commonly in connection with an athlete's skill. For the unfolding soul, agility is that alertness and presence of mind that you bring to every experience in the world.

Agility is that liveliness and promptness to show up with your soul, no matter what mood you might be in at the moment. The agile soul is also supple. Suppleness is the natural movement of the body, mind, and heart when working together as an ensemble.

Endurance is improved through the testing of endurance. Flexibility is enhanced through the testing of flexibility. Agility is increased through the testing of agility.

With endurance, flexibility, and agility now in your soul's wheelhouse, you are able to create new approaches to the problems of life as they manifest. Life in this world should not be about managing stress poorly but about learning how to reduce the negative effects of stress and using stress to the soul's best advantage. If in all things we learn to burn, then cool, build, then rest, we will grow steadily in the wisdom of soulful living.

In soul journey 24, you are led through a visualization technique in burning and cooling your energy. The stress of the world and within our minds can be reduced through this and similar meditation practices.

SOUL JOURNEY 24
Burn and Cool

MEDITATION

Find a place of quiet. Close your eyes. Enter your breathing room. First, take two strong breaths inhaling through your nose and exhaling out of your mouth. This will engage your mind and your body—a simple way to initiate presence, to be, here, now.

Next, naturally breathe. With your mind, inhale from the crown of your head, downward to your chest, then exhale into your stomach.

While repeating this, if thoughts intrude,gently note their existence, then return to your mindful practice. Do this for a several minutes if you wish.

AWAKENING EXERCISE

Notice how the racing thoughts in your mind mimic your daily life. They upset your apple cart at any given moment.

Right now, just leave all of them behind and concentrate on this one thought, "I am energy." Inhale "I am" and exhale "energy" three times. Feel your thoughts burn away when you focus your awareness on this truth of your soul.

Imagine playing with your energy as you would if you were sitting in a shallow pool and waving your arms ever so slowly and with ease through the water. Feel the water's cooling effect that contrasts with the heating effect of your arms and hands in motion.

Now, with open palms, pull the water up as you raise your hands and push the water down as you lower them. Feel the heat of your hands directing the flow of the water as they lift upward and feel the coolness when you relax your hands as they slowly descend.

Next, let your limbs move freely with the natural motion of the water. Feel them gently sway as the undulating water moves them as if they were floating branches. Breathe into this playful dance with the water until your arms and hands feel as light as a feather.

When you are finished, slowly open your eyes and become aware of your body and reconnect with your physical surroundings. Sense the energy all around you and within you.

Go into your day today with this sense that you are the epitome of burning and cooling energy in perfect rhythm and balance. Take responsibility for how you expend and conserve, burn and cool your precious energy as you go through your day. Welcome everything that comes.

CHAPTER 25

Meditation-in-Action

BRINGING A MEDITATIVE MIND to daily life is an art of rhythm and flow. A beginner in meditation will often say they're searching for balance, as if such a thing were an issue of time management. Actually, balance is more an attitude of calibrating and aligning to the heartbeat of our soul within everything thing we do. Real balance is connecting to the rhythm and flow of life that only a meditative mind and fully sensed soul can achieve.

Mindful action is a state of being, a condition of alert rest (meditation) and serene doing (action). We need to install it regularly into our lives like we do the washing of our bodies. A balanced rhythm of diving deep into being and stretching out into action will transform the darkness of negativity that lurks around every corner of the material world.

No matter how mature the soul, every seeker needs to attend to the silence of being before engaging in action. It takes a while before a meditator can bring a sense of calm into their waking hours, where the soul flows with every activity seamlessly in one movement.

There are only a few monasteries left in existence, at least in the West, which dedicate their lives to mindful action. As I've noted, it was there that I learned how to bring a meditative mind into daily life. In the sixth century CE, the renowned monk, Benedict of Nursia, based his order on a rule where "prayer and work" (ora et labora) is central.

Life was much simpler when I was a monk and my wristwatch was the bell gong of the abbey. I moved in attunement to the seasons of the forest and field, within a rhythm of solitary and communal living. I tasted honey from honeycombs; harvested corn, tomatoes, and rhubarb; tapped maple trees for syrup; bagged ripened apples; waded in streams to cut watercress; and skated across frozen lakes bundled up under a night sky full of stars.

A monk's ideal is to experience these moments—every moment, including scrubbing bathrooms, repairing walls, and sweeping floors—as one continuous prayer, one seamless meditation.

Meditation in action and action in meditation is the most difficult art to excel in, even in a monastic setting. And within a busy world, it becomes almost impossible. Finding spaces that are unplugged and unpolluted by noise to claim a few moments of quiet, or to even read a few ancient words of the wise before you fall asleep, is becoming increasingly difficult.

It is best to install a time of inner quiet in the morning, before your day begins. If you do this on the front end, you will be more likely to bring to the world a listening mind rather than a talking brain. The mind of the self incessantly talks. The mind of the soul always listens.

Whether you encounter a hundred people, a few, or none today, your mind, your consciousness, has the choice to take a minute's time to wash yourself in the light. Connecting with your soul is only two seconds away, the time it takes to become gratefully aware of your breathing. Once you accomplish this small but high priority task of soul hygiene, you will radiate light to this darkened world of shadows.

Right now, at this very second, no matter what time of day it is, there are monks, contemplative householders, and others who are practicing meditation and then flowing into mindful action. They have compassionate understanding of the matrix of the self that most of the world is trapped within.

These ever-wakeful ones have affection for you, even though they have not met you in physical form. Their prayers can help dissolve your negativity. All you have to do is to open yourself to their healing light and to the light of your own soul.

In soul journey 25, after connecting with the quiet flow of your breath, you will be guided in how to sense the quality of the flow within yourself and within nature. This exercise will help you move seamlessly from meditation into action and action into meditation.

SOUL JOURNEY 25
Sensing Flow

MEDITATION

Go to that place of quiet. Sit comfortably. Enter your breathing room. As you close your eyes incorporate the simple technique of "soft focus within," relaxing the muscles around your eyes, your forehead, around your mouth and your jaw, your neck, chest, and stomach.

Next, take two strong breaths inhaling through your nose and out your mouth. This will immediately connect your mind with your body and convey to you a sense of presence.

Now, breathe only through your nose. Breathe naturally and let your awareness follow your breath as the oxygen detoxes your body and you feel a clean sense of flow removing any mental obstruction.

Repeat this for ten cycles.

Awakening Exercise

Feel right now this fact: that all of creation—natural and manufactured—is filled with the energy of light. Imagine the flow of light energy within hard objects ... now, bring your attention to the flow of light energy within your dense body ... within your finite mind ... and finally, feel the flow of light energy within your infinite soul. This is your real breath.

Let this breath of light energy inundate every fiber of your being as you inhale the light from above your head and exhale down through the central column of your body to your feet and into the earth.

You are now one with the flow and connecting with the flow, with the great sense of your soul.

Keeping your eyes closed, imagine that you are reconnecting with all of your physical surroundings from this place. Breathe deeply into your core as you say silently, "I walk into every experience aware of this breath of light energy coursing through my entire being in one constant, rhythmic flow."

Today, take a few seconds to be entirely receptive to the flow of light within yourself and radiate the flow of this light quietly to every person, place, and thing around you.

Companionship with the Soul

AT THE CORE OF our existence lies an invaluable substance that we depend upon to nourish our souls and the souls of others. That substance is the heart of being. Within the heart of being reside all the higher senses of our soul.

When you travel to where the heart of being dwells, that place within, you are everywhere you need to be. Companionship with your soul creates the preconditions for expanded states of awareness and deeper love for others.

In the solitude of the soul, we are never alone. We experience emptiness as a nurturing and alive space. When solitude is received like a friend, the soul can sense a mysterious yet familiar sense of comfort and peace.

Let me suggest something to you now: that inside you dwells a smiling and serene monk. The inner monk is a name for our capacity to see with the kind eyes of our soul.

The inner monk symbolizes the soul's sense of seeing from within.

When we acquire this way of inner seeing, we move beyond opinions and beliefs as well as beyond the structures of all that can be perceived by the five senses. With the inner monk's sight we behold the mind of being, what some seers have described as a golden sea of light.

Inside you also dwells an inner mystic. Through the ages the mystic has been described as someone initiated in the mysteries of the inner world. In ancient times, an initiate of soul received an experience of reality behind appearances, of that oneness behind multiplicity. The mystic within embodies our capacity for that loving connection to the heart of being.

Both the inner monk and the inner mystic are what distinguish the personality of your self from the personality of your soul. The monk within represents your soul's pull into the mind of being. The mystic within represents your soul's pull into the heart of being. The heart of being gradually opens the seeker's heart with tenderness. The mind of being washes the seeker's heart with light.

This soul therapy can often correct certain mental and emotional states of imbalance. We find we are able to handle more challenges when our hearts are opened and we are cleansed with the energy of love. Anger, fear, and sorrow are seen for what they are: disturbed energy seeking intelligent affection.

When banded together, the monk and mystic emerge within the soul as a powerful synergy of the soul's senses of sight and touch, awareness and love. Love without awareness is blind. Awareness without love is cold. Together, awareness and love become a dynamo for the soul whether in solitude or among others in the material world.

The heart of being is love. The mind of being is awareness. The breath of the soul is spirit. Love and awareness form the principal organs of the soul that work together in order to breathe life into the organs of the physical body.

When we expand love and awareness within ourselves, we will naturally extend that love and awareness to others in the world. By making friends with our soul through solitude, we are better prepared to join the circle of humanity with more enthusiasm and vigor.

When the forces of awareness and love are united and working together, they allow the embodied soul to unfold into higher states of consciousness and to exhibit the joy of living soulfully in the world.

In soul journey 26, you are invited to activate your inner monk and inner mystic. These are archetypes—living forces within the soul—that represent the embodiment and outpouring of awareness and love.

SOUL JOURNEY 26
Contacting the Monk and Mystic Within

MEDITATION

Find a fitting place of quiet. Sit comfortably and close your eyes. Enter your breathing room. Raising your shoulders, take two strong breaths, inhaling through your nose and exhaling through your mouth. You are present now to this moment.

Next, begin inhaling and exhaling deeper and deeper into your heart. When you inhale, imagine the oxygen—turned into spirit—trickling into your heart. When you exhale, imagine the oxygen—turned into spirit—soaking your heart.

Continue for ten breath cycles.

AWAKENING EXERCISE

Drink in the silence of listening, watching, and waiting for the appearance of your inner monk.

Imagine what this being looks like. Feel free to color in and alter any image that floats up into your awareness until a portrait resonates with your own personal ideal of the affectionate seer.

Give yourself the permission to follow your inner monk and look within. Accept any darkness or light that you may happen to "see" with your eyes closed. Look into the mind of your being with the light of your soul.

Now, imagine that your inner mystic is present in this atmosphere of watching and waiting. Feel the warmth this being represents, total unconditional acceptance of life. Feel the heart of your being cleanse and uphold you.

Give yourself the permission to resonate with your inner mystic, feeling the presence of love within you.

Open your eyes and feel the atmosphere of your inner monk and inner mystic pervading the room.

This spirit you are breathing in and out is full of intelligent love and loving intelligence. This practice activates your inner monk and inner mystic. Feel free to use them if or whenever you need to attach an image to awareness and love.

Throughout the day, as you breathe in and out naturally, visualize this loving awareness and aware love within you, extending to everyone around you.

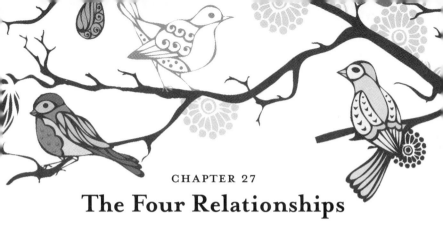

CHAPTER 27

The Four Relationships

AS THE SEEKER BECOMES more intimate with their soul, they can better determine the health of their relationships and encourage their evolution.

THE LIMITED RELATIONSHIP

Childhood playmates, classmates, workmates, and even partners can live alongside one another for years, knowing one another primarily by what they do together. Many rarely connect with each other at the deeper level of being. There is a built-in ceiling in such relationships because there is an investment in maintaining the status quo. Absent are strategies of assessment, what works and what does not, requests for change, or open discussions on how to end the relationship if warranted. There are marriages of duty, and then there are marriages of soul.

The Neutral Relationship

What most frequently typifies a neutral relationship is a conscious or unconscious desire to neglect it. If left unattended, for instance, a friendship can morph into a gray zone of disconnection, where even physical contact has been put on hold. When a relationship has moved from a limited to a neutral state, there may be only one who senses the estrangement that has occurred. Often disinterest or avoidance keep a neutral relationship from receiving the nurture or the closure it needs for both to move on. Once we are made aware of our soul's path, we will know the best way to move forward.

The Toxic Relationship

When two people attract one another's weaknesses with a fiery intensity, heaven can transform into hell. The toxic relationship is characterized by an all-pervasive atmosphere of negative stress. Dramas abound. Physical, mental, or emotional abuse can hold a person captive for years. Illness and even death may result unless an escape strategy is implemented. Fear of change may become the primary reason that someone remains stuck in a destructive attachment. Only the soul knows the difference between what bonds and what binds.

The Unlimited or Evolving Relationship

There is a fourth kind of connection that has an entirely different quality and lifeline. The main feature of the unlimited relationship is a mutual desire for individual and interpersonal growth. There is a willingness to learn how to healthfully communicate. There are struggles and growing pains, but the presence of mutual regard triumphs. The sky is the limit.

Conscious souls on a growth path are allies, not adversaries. There is equality in consciousness and vibration. Wakeful souls can navigate change with less emotional pain. It is the nature of intelligent love to expand and unfold and wish the same for all concerned.

If both are willing to find soulful purpose in and through loving each other, a relationship can be re-envisioned and strategies for renewal implemented.

Nature seems to know the right amount of space and the right amount of closeness needed to thrive. The same applies to human relationships. Earth nature appears to do a much better job than human nature in this endeavor.

Two souls on a growth path and in touch with their soul natures, however, thrive on mutual support and encouragement to become their best selves.

LESSONS OF LOVE

Regardless of the kind of relationship you find yourself in, the important thing is to become soul conscious. From the perspective of the unfolding soul, all relationships—even limited, neutral, or toxic ones—fulfill a purpose.

All relationships are full of teachings. What is required is listening to our soul to learn what is being asked of us. Once we have learned the lesson, it is unlikely it will come back to be repeated.

Do not judge yourself if a relationship has exhausted or bored you and you have decided to leave it because you feel it will hamper your growth.

Do not judge yourself if you have decided to stay in a limited relationship. Despite a narrow range of shared inner richness, if you are an evolving and unfolding soul, you won't use that as an excuse not to flourish. You will find other channels and other relationships to stretch and move you inward and upward.

Do not judge yourself if you find yourself stuck or paralyzed in a relationship that has become toxic. If this is the case, you must seek professional help. A skilled practitioner can sit with you and encourage you to listen to your heart and make decisions in your soul's best interest.

Perhaps an inner voice will convey to you whether or not you have completed a difficult task that love has given you. Only then will you know whether or not it is time to go. Love never dies. Love only changes form.

In soul journey 27, you are invited to reflect, not with your material mind, but with your soul mind, on where you are in each of your relationships. Learn what each is asking for and bring the energy of positivity to this process.

SOUL JOURNEY 27
Soul Mirrors

MEDITATION

Find a fitting place of quiet in an uncluttered space. Close your eyes as you sit to center yourself. Enter your breathing room within. Take two strong breaths, inhaling through your nose and exhaling through your mouth. This will give you a sense of immediate presence to the here and now.

Next, breathe through your nose naturally, following the rise and fall of your breath as you inhale cool oxygen and exhale warm carbon dioxide from your nostrils. Now, bring your attention to your heart, allowing your thoughts and feelings to come and go without attaching to them. Set them free. With your inner eye, see them untangle and stretch outward, disappearing into the expanse.

AWAKENING EXERCISE

Bring to mind your closest personal relationship. Give it the nutrients it needs for its growth. Pour light into it, and give it the warmth of encouragement and energy of purpose.

Do the same for all of your relationships and with those outside your immediate circle.

Engage your awareness with the inhalation and exhalation of your breath. While doing so, briefly recall the features of the four kinds of relationships: limited, neutral, toxic, and unlimited. Ask yourself which one seems dominant in the relationship most important to you right now. Bring the light of your soul to illuminate your situation, to give you the wisdom to know how best to approach this relationship with the tools you are acquiring.

Now do the same with yourself. What kind of relationship with yourself appears to be the dominant one? Is it unlimited, limited, neutral, or toxic? Allow the truth of where you live within yourself to surface. Accept whatever comes with the soul sense of compassion.

Open your eyes and reconnect with your surroundings. As you go about your day today, be conscious of how you project positivity or negativity to everyone you meet.

CHAPTER 28

The Great Romance

OUR SOUL'S BEING IS enlarged through the sharing of itself with others. Relationships are a spiritual path. When you fall in love and that love is shared equally, all of your senses are opened and your cup is filled. Everything comes alive. Colors, textures, tastes, sounds, and smells are experienced in a higher vibration. Every one of your soul's senses is lit up.

If more people understood the significance of that moment when love dawns, more would be awakened to their essence and find themselves on the path of soul awakening. When in love, we behold a new sun and moon in the sky. People and places we previously found unappealing or even ugly are now seen in a different light, in the aura of love. Love is always trying to get the attention of the soul because only the soul knows what to do with love.

If your love for another is soul-based, you will open again to love's embrace, no matter how much love has wounded you. The soulful lover knows that the heart is deepened, raised, and expanded through love's arrows. A soul conscious couple is able to attune to the chord of that lost harmony and resonate once again to a higher frequency and is willing to go wherever that music is taking them.

The wakeful soul welcomes love, whenever love comes and in whatever form love manifests. The soulful lover understands something of the mystery of love's mountainous path. Like the way of the sun and moon that makes all things flourish, love's unceasing play of hide and seek, conceal and reveal, enlivens the soulful lover. They know that love is only trying to make the soul larger by planting the seeds of longing. Longing stretches the heart. The soul knows this.

The soulful lover is never aloof. They do not need to protect themselves from love's risks. The soulful lover has no need to please others in hopes to diminish their chances of loss.

The soulful lover has no fear of their heart being broken, because they know that the heart of the soul is never broken, only opened and stretched to accommodate more love.

The soulful lover has no need to place their trust in others for they have placed their trust where it belongs, in the heart of love itself. Having placed their trust in love itself, there is no need to wear armor. To do so would be to block the light of love whose purpose is to melt armor.

The moment love touches us we know something magnificent has entered us, made its way into us. Become a soulful lover, and you won't need to control the lifeline of love nor the different shapes love will take.

What bliss awaits the soul that knows that the yearning for love's next touch and those cherished moments of love's ecstasy are ours to keep and to hold. We must let go of everything and everyone we love if we are to unfold to love's greater mystery and to the profound role love plays in our soul's destiny.

The self cannot contain love because its heart is too small. Only the soul can accommodate love. Small hearts produce small love. Big hearts produce big love. Love shows its exquisite face in every romance of the soul. Soulful love is the epitome of true romance.

Only when the self becomes a servant to its soul can the soul become a true servant to love. Every romance, in fact, is the soul's way of accomplishing its freedom from self, embraced by the oceanic arms of love.

Love's secret purpose is to dissolve all that blocks love. In this way the soul can unfold into the farthest reaches of love's endless horizon.

In soul journey 28, we are led to visualize the expansion of the heart. The goal of this exercise is see into one of the mysteries of love, the profound meaning of its sacred play of hide and seek.

SOUL JOURNEY 28
Expanding the Heart

MEDITATION

Seek out a space to sit quietly for a few moments before your day begins or during a break if you are at work.

Close your eyes and enter your breathing room. Take two strong breaths, big enough to feel your chest expand. This will help you arrive in your awareness to a concrete form of presence, where your mind joins with a movement of energy inside your body.

Follow the rise and fall of your breath in your own natural way and feel the uniqueness of each inhale and exhale.

With the tips of your fingers massage the outer ridges of your chest nearest to your solar plexus as deeply as you can tolerate, and then pull away slightly. Do this for ten breath cycles.

AWAKENING EXERCISE

As you inhale, imagine a spiral of heaven energy pouring down from above your head in a clockwise motion to your heart and a spiral of earth energy rising from the earth in a counterclockwise motion to your heart as well. As you exhale, feel your inner heart opening vertically and horizontally in depth, in breadth and in height. Do this for ten breath cycles.

Next, begin inhaling from the center of your heart and exhaling energy outward from your heart to the soul of a person you love. That person does not have to be physically present. Give that person spaciousness and light, wishing only their liberation from all suffering, fulfillment of their purpose and serenity. Continue this extension of good will to any and all with whom you struggle, including all beings on this earth.

When you are finished, open your eyes. Take in the protection of the energy surrounding you and pervading the room.

At a chosen time in your day today, take but a minute of inner quiet. With eyes opened or closed, draw in this positive energy from earth and heaven to your heart, and exhale this energy from your heart, extending it outward to someone whom you feel needs this.

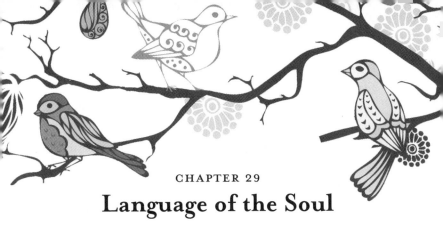

CHAPTER 29

Language of the Soul

FROM THE MOMENT OUR soul's journey on this earth begins, we bring to it the language of feeling. We sense love's presence as well as love's absence in every gesture, every touch, every taste, every smell, and every sound.

Mind speaks the language of mind. Heart speaks the language of heart. Body speaks the language of body. Spirit speaks the language of spirit. Soul speaks every language.

If someone close speaks the language of the body, the soul will give needed space or a warm embrace.

If another speaks the language of the mind, the soul will give freedom of ideas.

If another speaks the language of the heart, the soul will give empathy and understanding.

If another speaks the language of action, the soul will give usefulness.

If another speaks the language of beauty, the soul will give what for them is lovely to behold.

If another speaks the language of struggle, the soul will give calm and comfort.

The language of the soul is every word of depth written upon the scrolls of time and every note of joy and sorrow played on drum, horn, and string.

The language of the soul speaks in the silence amidst the swaying caravans of travelers through the hills under moonlit skies. The soul's voice breaks into a thousand little suns shimmering upon the surface of the sea in serene mornings of solitude.

The language of the soul is born of heaven and the earth, of water and of fire.

The language of the soul is the movement of worm and stem according to the horizontal and vertical lines of growth, revealing the secret of evolution until it reaches human existence.

The language of the soul is every step of the rising ego until, reaching the top if its stair, it delivers itself to that infinity that only the blooming flower of a soul and blooming soul of a flower can reach.

Each of the senses of the soul conveys its own language of awakening.

The soul's sense of sight sees a kingdom in an atom and a seed in a far off universe.

The soul's sense of touch resonates with the pulse of the earth and the vibration of a star.

The soul's sense of hearing attunes to the hum of bees and the music of the spheres.

The soul's sense of smell delights in the aroma of musk and in the scent of the saint.

The soul's sense of taste savors the milk of meditation and the wine of bliss.

The language of the soul is the sanatana dharma, the eternal teaching of the paths and their yogas.

The language of the soul expresses all the ways of love made upon the beds of heaven and earth.

The language of the soul speaks through the moans of the lover, the chants of the monk, the kirtans of the Sufi, and the duende of the gypsy.

The language of the soul is in the whimper of the pup, in the roar of the lion, in the hiss of the serpent, and in the flap of the bird's wing.

The language of the soul is in the trickle of the stream and in the torrent of the flood.

The language of the soul is in the dance of Shakti and Shiva and celebrates the ecstasy of their intertwining.

The language of the soul is the force of light and the light within all force, interlocked light and fluid light, knotted light and released light.

The language of the soul is tangled love and spacious love, trapped loved and flowing love.

Make no mistake. The language of the soul is identical to its essence, always light, always love, light and love at rest, light and love moving, from and toward the very source of light.

Yes, the soul speaks every language.

In soul journey 29, you are asked to choose your favorite soul language. Calling someone to mind who is close to you and discerning which soul language they may have a kinship with will deepen your relationship with them.

SOUL JOURNEY 29
Expressing the Soul

MEDITATION

Find a fitting place to get away. Sit quietly, close your eyes, and enter your breathing room within. Take two strong breaths, inhaling through your nose and exhaling through your mouth. This method connects your mind with your body and helps to give you a sense of immediate presence.

Next, inhale through your nose and exhale into your core, about two finger widths below your navel. With your awareness follow the descent of your breath into your core. Do this for ten cycles or more, or until you are in the silence mode of listening with your soul.

AWAKENING EXERCISE

As you rest in the silence, reflect on what your favorite language is to express your soul to others.

Is it through the language of your body, through gesture and touch? Imagine yourself with someone you love expressing yourself in this way.

Is it through your mind, through the sharing of ideas? See yourself having an enthusiastic conversation of mutual regard.

Is it through your heart, through the sharing of feeling? Visualize yourself with another in total acceptance of where both of you are emotionally.

Once you complete this exercise, bring to mind the closest person to you. Imagine what their favorite language of the soul might be and respond to them in that language in your own way. At your first opportunity share this exercise with them and see whether they express themselves more with the language of the body, the mind, or the heart.

Today, picture yourself interacting with others from a place of acceptance and with an attitude of openness to understanding the language of their own unique soul.

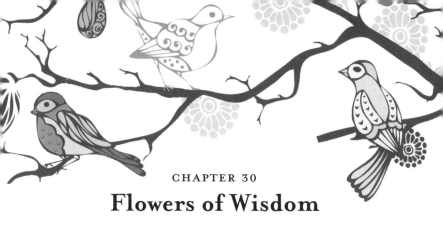

CHAPTER 30

Flowers of Wisdom

THE ANCIENT TEACHINGS OF the great soul mentors are garlands, fragrant reminders of the eternal blossoming of soul happening now within each of us. They instruct us where to search for God: within. They provide universal wisdom, maps for the soul's journey through the material world.

When we recall any guide that has trekked a distance with us on the inner road, we have little doubt that we are on a profound pilgrimage through this world. A pilgrimage takes the soul in two directions, vertical and horizontal, inward and outward. In this way the soul grows its consciousness, eventually, to discover the intimate interconnectivity of all things.

The Western symbols of the flower and the cross, for instance, both signify depth as well as expansion. For the self, now awakened to its essence, the cross becomes a compass to direct the way of the soul. As the soul mind continues to infinitely unfold, it both deepens vertically and expands horizontally. Look at a flower and superimpose the cross. Look at a cross and superimpose a flower, a tree, or anything that grows in nature and you will understand the life of the soul on earth.

The Eastern symbol of the lotus with its countless petals is also a pictorial representation of the flowering aspect of the soul. The soul is hardwired to eventually experience infinite being (sat), infinite consciousness (chit), and infinite bliss (ananda) in every moment of this life.

Satchitananda is the eternal teaching from the great soul mentors of ancient days that conveys to the seeker the very nature of the soul: that the soul is being, that the soul is consciousness, and that the soul is bliss.

A great soul mentor manifests satchitananda in its completeness. Total enlightenment is the continual and unceasing experience of the fully unfolded soul knowing itself as love and light, as infinite being, infinite consciousness, and infinite bliss.

Even the material mind experiences satchitananda, though in its shadow forms. The material mind mimics infinite being by the various ways it uses to extend its physical life in the body. Likewise, the material mind believes it can possess infinite consciousness through the acquisition of knowledge to gain power over others.

The seeking for pleasure by any means is the way that the material mind searches to gain infinite bliss, only to relinquish itself through illness, disease, and death. However, only the fully awakened soul can achieve the unceasing state of satchitananda that terminates the endless wheel of suffering.

Satchitananda defines what serenity is—a state of being. It is the energized and dynamic peace that comes with living a life of soul right now as it unfurls to its full potential. Serenity, like enlightenment, is also a process. The serenity of satchitananda is as much a state of becoming as it is a state of being.

Once the material mind learns to relegate itself to the leadership of the soul mind, a channel immediately opens to access the vast terrain of soul. The awakening process begins here, in that wondrous moment when the self first becomes conscious of itself as an individual soul.

Eastern wisdom explains it this way. The soul (atma) is limitless. When the soul takes a body and must utilize its brain and nervous system to function in the world, it has become an embodied soul (jivatma). The jivatma's path is toward becoming a fully realized soul (shivatma) by reuniting with its origin and source (paramatma).

The beyond soul (paramatma) also exists within the embodied soul (jivatma) as the inmost self (purusha). These are not ideas or concepts but ancient teachings meant to provide a picture of the all-pervasiveness of soul as the one reality. This one reality can be experienced once the senses of the soul have been awakened and strengthened.

Through the meditation technique of focused breathing with kind awareness, oxygen becomes spirit, warmed by the soul's touch. Through visualization, your material mind connects with your soul mind, expanded by the soul's sense of sight. Through affirmation, consciousness attunes to our inmost self through the soul's hearing.

The yogas enable the golden flower of the soul to grow and strengthen within the physical body. The inmost self funnels nutrients to the soul and the soul funnels nutrients to the body and mind. These nutrients are light and love. Every soul is a golden bud of energy, blossoming into a being composed of light and love. Every soul is a unique embodiment of satchitananda on its way to perfection.

From the moment the soul takes a physical body, it awaits to be fed light and love like the flowers and plants of earth await the sun and rain. As you place more attention upon your soul and trust in its desire, the bud of your soul opens and becomes a blossoming flower. This blossoming flower is composed of infinite light and infinite love. This is your true essence. This is your true existence. This is your true becoming. This is your true being.

In soul journey 30, you are led to visualize your inmost self by recalling those teachers and teachings that have crossed your path up to this point in your journey. This exercise deepens your appreciation of the key role soul mentors play in your life. They connect you with your inner teacher, your inmost self, and provide you with maps and means that will guide you as you continue to make your way along your path.

SOUL JOURNEY 30
Contacting Your Inmost Self

MEDITATION

Locate a fitting space where you can find a few moments of inner quietude. Sit comfortably. Close your eyes and enter your breathing room, that place within that radiates spacious love. Raise your shoulders and take two strong breaths, inhaling through your nose and exhaling from your mouth. This will convey to you an immediate sense of presence, of consciousness in your body.

Next, begin your nasal breathing into your core. As you inhale, gently pull your breath from your head into your heart, and as you exhale, softly push your breath from your heart into the navel area of your lower abdomen. Bring your awareness to the gradual deepening of your breath. Do this for ten or more breath cycles.

Awakening Exercise

As you continue this subtle deep breathing exercise, call to mind any and all teachers and teachings you have encountered thus far on your path of life. They might be parents, friends, mentors, or partners. As you think of each, take all that energy into your core. This energy is light and love.

Allow yourself to sit in the presence of this energy. Imagine this energy commingling with your wise and loving inmost self that is always present and always available to you.

This inmost self is the essence within you. Your inmost self is always there to nurture you and unfold your soul through infinite light and infinite love. All you have to do is consciously connect with your essence to activate this light and love.

Take a few moments every day to sense with your soul this illumined and radiant presence, this flower that gives you the energy of serenity, that enlivening peace that flows like a stream of fresh water.

Trust that you are being guided every step of the way as you continue to embody and unfold this presence within yourself, becoming who you are—an eternal flower of wisdom.

Conclusion

THIS AWE-INSPIRING UNIVERSE IS a school of higher learning, a place of continual development and unfoldment. The self develops. Then, after the self's summit of growth has been attained, the soul can take over where the self left off to unfold to its full potential. We evolve, and then we unfold. And we keep unfolding. This is the great journey.

As wayfarers on the great pilgrimage through this earth, we know that our world path and our soul path have finally merged. We know that world needs soul and that soul needs world.

Although our path may change and we might take many detours, we have come to experience that even those side streets are part of the journey. We know that we have many more awakenings before us as we continue to become ever more soul purposed in our seeking.

We are living in a time unequaled in the history of humanity. As yet unreachable by physical means, all points have become virtually attainable. Worldwide networking is now instantaneous.

It is indisputable that genuine connection must begin with the soul, because true relation is an inside job. The reality of the soul and the unreality of the self has always been one of the best-kept secrets no matter what historical time period emerges and passes. Perhaps it has always been this way. Of course, the truth of soul is not a secret kept from someone. It is a secret that is revealed as soon as someone is ready to receive it.

There are many reasons the soul has come to this earth, yet there is an overarching reason, a reason for being. Living as a monk, I sought to find serenity and soulful purpose through the study of ancient wisdom from the East and West. Yet I had no inkling then where this road would lead me.

The world will always need pathways to connect with soul beyond what doctrinal proclamations can convey: that the essence of you, the essence of the universe, is the only reality.

My purpose in offering thirty soul journeys in this book has been to help you connect to your body, to your heart, and to your mind, from the perspective of your soul; from your true essence. You can experience this essence, the epicenter of your being, through the threefold practice of meditation, affirmation, and visualization. These are tools for the soul; when sharpened and used on a regular basis, they will transform your way of being in the world. And the world will be made better for it.

When we move from being self-centered to soul-centered, we begin, again and again, each and every day, from the place of presence. The present moment is the epicenter of being. The epicenter is that place from which all relevant and real activity arises. What is important is not what you do but how you do what you do, from what inner place you act. What is important is not what you think but how you think, from what inner place you think. It is not important what you say but how you say what you say, from what inner place you speak.

In our journey through the teachings of this book, let the meditations and awakening exercises lead you ever more inward and outward, toward embodiment and unfoldment. Continue to align your kind awareness with your breath, to center yourself in being, in your soul, and never stop living in the world from that place.

In this way you will cultivate soul intelligence. Soul intelligence is enhanced whenever you activate and empower your inner senses, faculties of your soul that were once dormant but are now alive.

You must first find the peace within you that the world cannot give before you can extend that peace to others. When we see earth and all of its inhabitants as a lively place where all are called to make total sense of the soul, then living a soulful life will become an utterly full life.

Continue to learn how to grow your soul in the material world by paying more attention to who and what you really are. Though the path is long from ignorance to enlightenment, this earth is a magnificent arena, the perfect place for the soul to make this journey of journeys.

No matter how far you may have come in making sense of your soul, receive this secret about yourself. Every true seeker is the dweller, the questioner, the wanderer, the aspirant, the wayfarer, and the soul mentor. All of us are all of these, some in seed, some in bud, some in flower. All of us, the entire creation, are mirrors of one another, mirrors of light and love. Everyone, everything, and every moment present teachings of wisdom.

Learn to dwell more and more in being. Question what is behind you rather than what is before you. Wander, seek, and find new treasures within your soul and within the souls of others. Aspire to expand your heart until it encompasses the universe. Through the refined soul senses of empathy, compassion, and forgiveness, impart this healing balm to others in the world, beginning with yourself.

There is an abundant store of soul knowledge yet to be revealed to you. As you continue along your path of awakenings, know that love and light are always with you, guiding you from that deep place within you and above you. The journey continues.

Recommended Reading

Bourgeault, Cynthia. *Centering Prayer and Inner Awakening.* Lanham, MD: Cowley Publications, 2004.

Brown, Joseph Epes. *The Sacred Pipe: Black Elk's Account of the Seven Rites of the Oglala Sioux.* Originally published in 1953. Norman, OK: University of Oklahoma, 1989.

Easwaran, Eknath, translator. *The Bhagavad Gita.* Tomales, CA: Nilgiri Press, 2007.

———. *The Upanishads.* Petaluma, CA: Nilgiri Press, 1987.

Feuerstein, George, translator. *The Yoga-Sutra of Patanjali: A New Translation and Commentary.* Rochester, VT: Inner Traditions International, 1989.

Goldberg, Philip. *American Veda: From Emerson and the Beatles to Yoga and Meditation, How Indian Spirituality Changed the West.* New York: Harmony, 2010.

Goswami, Shyam Sundar. *Layayoga: The Definite Guide to the Chakras and Kundalini*. Rochester, VT: Inner Traditions, 1999.

Griffin, Albert Kirby. *Religious Proverbs*. Jefferson, NC: MacFarland, 1991.

Hazrat Inayat Khan. *The Soul Whence and Whither*. London: East-West Publications, 1984.

———. *Complete Works of Pir-O-Murshid Hazrat Inayat Khan. Original Texts: Lectures on Sufism. 1923 II: July-December*. London: East-West Publications, 1982.

Heschel, Abraham Joshua. *Who Is Man?*. Stanford, CA: Stanford University Press, 1965.

Hillman, James. *The Soul's Code: In Search of Character and Calling*. New York: Warner, 1996.

Isaacson, Walter. *Einstein: His Life and Universe*. New York: Simon & Schuster, 2007.

Jessawala, Eruch. *The Ancient One*. Edited by Naosherwan Anzar. Englishtown, NJ: Beloved Books, 1985.

Katz, Vernon, and Thomas Egenes, translators. *The Upanishads: A New Translation*. New York: Jeremy P. Tarcher, 2015.

Ladinsky, Daniel, translator. *Hafiz: The Subject Tonight Is Love*. Myrtle Beach, SC: Pumpkin House Press, 1996.

Ladinsky, Daniel, translator. *Love Poems From God: Twelve Sacred Voices from the East and West*. New York: Penguin, 2002.

Meher Baba. *God Speaks: The Theme of Creation and Its Purpose*. Second Edition. New York: Dodd, Mead & Company, 1973.

Meisel, Anthony, translator. *The Rule of St. Benedict*. Originally written in Latin in the sixth century CE. New York: Image Books, 1975

Neihardt, John G, editor. *Black Elk Speaks: Being the Life Story of a Holy Man of the Oglala Sioux*. Lincoln: University of Nebraska, 1971.

Sargeant, Winthrop, translator. *The Bhagavad Gita*. Albany, NY: State University of New York Press, 2009.

Satprem. *Sri Aurobindo or The Adventure of Consciousness*. New York: Discovery Publisher, 2005.

Sri Aurobindo. *The Synthesis of Yoga*. Originally Published in 1921. Twin Lakes, WI: Lotus Press, 1996.

Star, Jonathan. *Two Suns Rising: A Collection of Sacred Writings*. New York: Bantam Books, 1991.

Stevens, John. *Abundance Peace: The Biography of Morihei Ueshiba, Founder of Aikido*. Boulder, CO: Shambhala Publications, 1987.

Trungpa, Chögyam. *Shambhala: The Sacred Path of the Warrior*. New York: Bantam, 1988.

Tyberg, Judith M. *The Language of the Gods*. Los Angeles: East-West Cultural Centre, 1970.

Vivekananda, Swami. *Bhakti-Yoga: The Yoga of Love and Devotion*. Original publication unknown. Kolkata, India: Advaita Ashrama, 2017.

———. *Karma-Yoga*. Originally published in 1933. Mansfield Center, CT: Martino Publishing, 2012.

———. *Raja-Yoga*. Originally published in 1956. New York: Ramakrishna-Vivekananda Center, 1982.

Wilson, Andrew, editor. *World Scripture. A Comparative Anthology of Sacred Texts*. New York: Paragon House, 1995.

Zohar, Danah. *SQ: Connecting With Our Spiritual Intelligence*. New York: Bloomsbury Press, 2000.

Glossary

Ascending Knowledge (Aroha-pantha) (Sanskrit): In Indian philosophy, the path of argument and reason.

Aiki/Aikido (Japanese): The Japanese term *aiki* means "harmonious energy" or "the power of love." *Ai* means "love" or "harmony" and *ki* means "energy" or "power." *Aikido* means the "way" (*do*) of "harmonizing" (*ai*) "energy" (*ki*). Morihei Ueshiba was the founder of the martial art of Aikido, a Japanese form of self-defense that uses locks, holds, throws, and the opponent's own movements to neutralize and harmonize the energy of the parties engaged.

Bhakti Yoga (Sanskrit): Also called *bhakti marga*, literally the "path of bhakti," it is a spiritual way that focuses on loving devotion to a personal deity or living master.

It is one of the three major paths, leading to soul-realization. The others are jnana and karma yoga.

Bodhisattva (Sanskrit): In the Mahayana ("greater vehicle") tradition of Buddhism prominent in north Asia, a bodhisattva refers to a person who has generated *bodhicitta*, a spontaneous wish and compassionate mind to attain Buddhahood (enlightenment) for the benefit of all sentient beings.

Breath Control (Pranayama) (Sanskrit): In Indian yogas, *pran* ("breath") *ayama* ("restraint" or "control") is the regulation of the breath through certain techniques and exercise.

Buddha (Sanskrit): A Buddhist term that literally means "awakened one." It also refers to Siddhartha Gautama, the figure around which Buddhism eventually emerged. When Master Gautama passed around 500 BCE, his disciples organized a religious movement that would develop into Buddhism.

Chakra (Sanskrit): Literally "wheel" or "circle," *chakra* refers to the various energy centers or focal points in the subtle body used in a variety of ancient meditation practices.

Charis (Greek): Literally "grace, kindness, and life."

Charism (Greek): A power or talent believed to be divinely conferred.

Circling Forward (Pravritti) (Sanskrit): Literally, "to circle forward," *pravritti* signifies the outward movement of the material mind in the manifesting of form in the material universe.

Circling Inward (Nivritti) (Sanskrit): Literally means, "to circle inward," and denotes the direction of awareness with the breath in meditation.

Descending Knowledge (Avaroha-pantha) (Sanskrit): In Indian philosophy, *avaroha-pantha* is the process of descending knowledge, the path of surrender.

Dharma (Sanskrit): In Indian religions, *dharma* is the eternal and inherent nature of reality, the cosmic law and teaching of the Buddha undergirding religion and social order.

Duende (Spanish): Literally meaning "ghost," *duende* is a term often used in the Spanish music of flamenco, meaning a heightened state of emotion, expression, and authenticity.

Embodied Soul (Jivatma/Jivatman) (Sanskrit): The term *jivatma* comes from the Sanskrit, *jiv* (to breathe) and *atma* (soul), ensouled self. In Indian philosophy, *jivatma* means the individual, embodied, or enfleshed soul.

Energy Centers (Dantien) (Chinese): *Dantien* is loosely
translated as "elixir field," "sea of chi," or simply
"energy flow center." There are primarily three energy
flow centers: Upper dantien (*shen*) in the area of the
head, middle dantien (*chi*) in the chest area, and the
lower dantien (*jing*) in the area of the abdomen. The
three dantien are important focal points for meditative
and exercise techniques, such as qigong and tai chi and
in traditional Chinese medicine.

Hatha Yoga (Sanskrit): The word *hatha* comes from the
roots *ha* ("sun") and *tha* ("moon"). Hatha yoga refers
to a set of physical exercises and postures called *asanas*
designed to align the breath with the body; it also
includes breath control (*pranayama*) and meditation
(*dhyana*).

Infinite Intelligence (Nous) (Greek): In Greek philosophy,
"mind" (*nous*) denotes infinite intelligence or divine
reason. In Neo-Platonism, *nous* is regarded as the first
emanation of infinite intelligence as it descends to
the mind of human consciousness, then to its form
as energy, finally culminating in the creation of the
physical form of a human.

Inmost Self (Purusha) (Sanskrit): A word used to speak
of the "inmost self," "soul" or "true self," also the
"cosmic self" from which the universe is created.

This complex concept evolved in Vedic and Upanishadic times.

Insight Meditation (Vippasana) (Pali): Literally "inward vision," this is a meditation technique that involves concentration on the body or its sensations. However, the goal is insight into reality which arises from this practice.

Jnana Yoga (Sanskrit): Also known as *jnana marga*, it is one of the spiritual paths of ancient India that emphasizes the path of knowledge or the path of the mind. It is one of the three major paths leading to soul-realization; the two others are bhakti and karma yoga.

Kaa'ba (Arabic): A small stone building in the court of the Great Mosque at Mecca that contains a sacred black stone and is the goal of the Islamic pilgrimage, as well as the point toward which Muslims turn when praying.

Karma Yoga (Sanskrit): Also called karma marga, meaning the "path of (selfless) action," it is one of the three major paths to soul-realization.

Kirtan (Sanskrit): Refers to a genre of religious performance arts in India, connoting a musical form of narration or shared recitation, particularly of spiritual or religious ideas.

Kundalini (Sanskrit): Literally "coiled one" and has also been translated as "divine-light-energy." Located and "coiled" at the base of the spine, kundalini yoga focuses on practices to awaken kundalini energy.

Laya Yoga (Sanskrit): *Laya* means "to dissolve." The goal of laya yoga is the dissolution of the material mind and merging with infinite mind or supreme consciousness, achieved through attunement of the soul to universal energy.

Maya (Sanskrit): *Maya* signifies both illusion and the power that generates illusion. Illusion is understood as the manifest universe and the manifold phenomena that conceal the unity of being.

Meditation-in-Action (Ora et Labora) (Latin): The phrase *ora et labora* (meaning "prayer and work") refers to the Western monastic practice of meditation-in-action. It is generally associated with the sixth-century Rule of St. Benedict. St. Benedict of Nursia taught spiritual practices that sought to blend a monk's meditative life with daily action.

Monakhos (Greek): The word means "single" or "solitary"; the root, *monos*, means "alone." These words describe the "monk," considered an individual who is single and solitary. The esoteric meaning of *monakhos/*

monk denotes an individual that is on the path of yoga, of unifying all that is divided within.

Mystes (Greek): From *muo*, (plural *mystai*) "to close the mouth," in ancient Greece associated with the initiation into the first degrees of the mysteries (esoteric knowledge).

Prem Yoga (Sanskrit): A word that means "love." Prem yoga is considered to be the more intimate form of bhakti yoga. Both are devotional practices to a disembodied deity, such as Krishna, and the desire to receive that deity into the heart. Prem yoga is considered to be the most intimate and highest devotional practice, whereby the soul is entirely absorbed in love through taking the name of the Guru into one's heart.

Qigong/Ch'i Kung (Chinese): Literally "life-energy cultivation," is a holistic system of coordinated body postures and movements incorporating breathing and meditation techniques used for the purposes of health and the refinement of energy and consciousness.

Raja Yoga (Sanskrit): This yoga incorporates the meditative practice of concentrating the mind to access the innermost recesses of mind, the inmost self, or supreme soul. Breathing techniques, such as pranayama (or controlled breathing) are used.

Sanatana Dharma (Sanskrit): *Sanatana* means "eternal." Combined with *dharma*, it refers to the "eternal teaching," or the "eternal cosmic order."

Sangha (Sanskrit): The word *sangha* means "association," "assembly," or "community." The term is frequently associated with a more intimate group or "company" of friends focused on spiritually based support.

Sanskara/Samskara (Sanskrit): In Indian philosophy, *sanskaras* (or *samskaras*) are mental impressions, habitual potencies, or psychological imprints of thought and action patterns implanted in the deeper structure of a person's mind. Sanskaras form all of a person's hidden expectations, karmic impulses, and innate disposition, including one's sense of self-worth concealed in the subconscious.

Sanyasa Yoga (Sanskrit): This is the practice of internal renunciation of self-based desire for soul-based desire, making use of all available means.

Satchitananda (Sanskrit): A term in Indian philosophy representing the highest goal of all embodied souls: *sat* (infinite being), *chit* (infinite consciousness), and *ananda* (infinite bliss). Knowledge is being. Knowledge is structured in consciousness and consciousness is structured in being. Satchitananda is a grouping of concepts describing the attainment of soul-realization or complete infinite consciousness.

Soul-Realization: Often cited as self-realization or god-realization, this continuous and unceasing state represents the culmination of the soul's journey in evolution from ego development to the complete blossoming of the soul's unfoldment into the subtle and supramental inner planes until the soul attains satchitananda: infinite being, infinite consciousness, and infinite bliss.

Spiritus (Latin): *Spiritus* is Latin for "spirit," "wind," "breath," and "blowing."

Sufi (Arabic): An Arabic word, from *suf*, meaning "wool," derived from the woolen garments its followers traditionally wear. The Sufi seeks to find the truth of divine love and knowledge through personal experience of the Divine. Although culturally associated with the Muslim faith, a Sufi does not have to follow any religion to walk the Sufi path of divine love.

Subtle Consciousness: One who is subtle conscious has accessed the inner planes of energy.

Supramental Consciousness: One who is supramental conscious has accessed the inner planes where the structures of consciousness reside. One who is established in the supramental sees all things by the light of infinite consciousness.

Supreme Self (Paramatma) (Sanskrit): The "beyond soul" or the "supreme self" in Indian philosophy.

Tai Chi (Chinese): *Tai chi* is an ancient Chinese tradition that involves a series of flowing movements performed in a slow and focused manner accompanied by coordinated breathing. It includes various physical postures and breathing techniques along with meditation.

Tao (Chinese): Meaning "the Way," in Chinese philosophy it is the absolute principle underlying the universe, combining within itself the principles of yin and yang. The Tao is in harmony with the natural order.

Tantra Yoga (Sanskrit): *Tantra* means "to weave" or "to expand." Tantra yoga explores the subtle energies within the body and their connection to the universe and the principles of unifying apparent opposites. Tantra yoga incorporates conscious breathing practices, pranayama, and meditation. It may be practiced alone or with another. In both, the relationship between the self and others is enhanced.

Wu Wei/Wu Wei Wu (Chinese): A concept in Chinese
philosophy, *wu wei* literally means "not-doing." The
complete phrase, *wu wei wu* is thus "doing without
doing." This is the Taoist ideal regarding action, refer-
ring to actions that are perfectly natural, effortless, and
spontaneous. *Wu wei wu* and the Western monastic
practice of *ora et labora* ("meditative action") as well as
karma yoga (selfless action) in Indian philosophy are
similar in that all three emphasize naturalness, inner
quietude, and movement that arises from being.

Acknowledgments

I WISH TO THANK Amy Glaser, acquisitions editor of Llewellyn Worldwide, for seeing the potential in a manuscript that had not yet come to full flower, to the production editor, Laura Kurtz, and the entire team at Llewellyn.

Without Dr. Ruth McIntyre's painstaking micro- and macro-editing of the early manuscripts and search for the most fitting home for my work, this effort would not have reached the desk of Llewellyn in the timely way it did.

This book would not have been brought forth had it not been for Dr. Thomas James Hickey's training in the practical applications of the perennial wisdom traditions, meditation, the yogas, and their spiritual paths.

Dr. Jeanne Schul offered insightful feedback in the initial drafts. Suzanne Ledoux provided helpful suggestions for clarity of expression, especially in the last stages of the writing process.

I thank my wife and companion, Wen Lundgren, for our soulful conversations through the years and selfless service to our children. She has been for me a constant source of ideas. I am grateful for my mother, Antoinette, who courageously modeled to me how a person embraces life and all of its many challenges. My three loyal and loving sisters, Sharon, Lisa, and Maria, I wish to thank for their love and support throughout every twist and turn of my life. For William Courville, Jack and Helen Graham, David Bankston, Gary Miller, Daniel Ladinsky, and to all of my companions of soul, I give thanks for our many rich conversations on the subject of soul and its central role in the shaping of human destiny.

I have so much gratitude for the many students that I have been honored to hold space with over the years, whose stories have breathed life into these pages. I give special thanks to Andy and Greer Monin, as well as to Lidia Nistor, for their strong encouragement to put into written form some of my reflections on the vast subject of the soul.

Finally, I wish to give a deep bow to the timeless soul mentors of the spiritual journey, and to all monks, mystics, and contemplative householders everywhere—East and West. If it were not for these great ones who continue to keep the flame of awareness and love alive for all seekers and inner travelers, the light of humanity, and our dearest earth, sun, moon, and stars would have surely vanished long ago.

To Write to the Author

If you wish to contact the author or would like more information about this book, please write to the author in care of Llewellyn Worldwide Ltd. and we will forward your request. Both the author and publisher appreciate hearing from you and learning of your enjoyment of this book and how it has helped you. Llewellyn Worldwide Ltd. cannot guarantee that every letter written to the author can be answered, but all will be forwarded. Please write to:

Neale Lundgren PhD
℅ Llewellyn Worldwide
2143 Wooddale Drive
Woodbury, MN 55125-2989

Please enclose a self-addressed stamped envelope for reply,
or $1.00 to cover costs. If outside the U.S.A., enclose
an international postal reply coupon.

Many of Llewellyn's authors have websites with
additional information and resources.

For more information, please visit our website at
http://www.llewellyn.com.